The Official NHL
1980s
Quiz Book

The Official NHL 1980s Quiz Book

Edited by
Dan Diamond

Questions by
James Duplacey, Bob Borgen, and Tom Pickard

Research by
Ralph Dinger

M&S

Toronto   New York   London

CANADIAN CATALOGUING IN PUBLICATION DATA

Diamond, Dan
   The official NHL 1980s Quiz Book

ISBN 0–7710–0066-7

1. National Hockey League – Miscellanea.   I. Title.

GV847.8.N3D5 1993   796.962'04   C93-094851-3

Cover design by Sari Ginsberg
Typesetting by M&S

Cover photo credits (clockwise from top): Steve Yzerman (Denis Brodeur), Mario Lemieux, Patrick Roy (Bruce Bennett Studios), Mike Bossy (NHL Publishing), Wayne Gretzky (Bruce Bennett Studios)

Text photos: NHL Publishing

Printed and bound in Canada

McClelland & Stewart
The Canadian Publishers
481 University Avenue
Toronto, Ontario
M5G 2E9

1 2 3 4 5   97 96 95 94 93

Contents

Note: Special quizzes and puzzles are scattered throughout the book.

Dear Jan
Will you be memorizing
all of this??
Much love Auntie Vanesa
Dec '99

❶

The Record Book

THE NHL GUIDE AND RECORD BOOK WAS REWRITTEN in the 1980s, with much of the editing being done by Wayne Gretzky and the Edmonton Oilers. Gretzky became the most dominant player in the history of team sport during the 1980s. No player ever established more records at a quicker pace than the Great One. Gretzky set or tied over 50 individual NHL marks, including a couple thought to be untouchable, such as Gordie Howe's all-time points and assists records. Some critics pointed to expansion resulting in a lessened on-ice product, but that is only a small fraction of the whole story. With the NHL opening its doors to Europe, the Soviet Union, and the college system, more skilled players entered the league in the 1980s than in any previous decade. These players were bigger, stronger, and faster, resulting in more offence and higher scores.

The Oilers completely altered the way the game was played during the decade, combining a run-and-gun offence with a strategic defence. Edmonton became the first team to score more than 400 goals in a season, a feat they accomplished in four consecutive seasons. In three of those seasons, the Oilers had four different players with at least 100 points. Not surprisingly, the Oilers also set a record where for four straight seasons four players scored at least 40 goals apiece, an awesome display of offensive domination.

In the 1980s, the best players from Europe joined the NHL, providing the league with skilled players who effectively combined savvy and finesse. The Stastny brothers – Anton, Peter and Marion – transformed the Quebec Nordiques into instant winners. Jari Kurri and Esa Tikkanen were key members of the Oilers' championship teams, while other European stars like Jaroslav Pouzar, Willy Lindstrom, Anders Kallur, and Stefan Persson were efficient role players with the Oilers' and Islanders' dynasties in the 1980s.

At the end of the decade, 43 team records in the NHL record book had been set in the 1980s, including most powerplay goals in a season, most goals in one game, most goals in one period, longest road winning streak, and longest losing streak. The individual categories belonged to Gretzky, but other players made their mark in the performance ledger. Mike Bossy of the Islanders scored 50 goals in nine straight seasons while Jari Kurri set a mark for goals by a right-winger. Defenceman Paul Coffey scored an incredible 48 goals and Tim Kerr of Philadelphia slammed home 34 powerplay goals in 1985-86.

The accent on scoring coupled with the continued emergence of offensive defencemen made an NHL goaltender's job a difficult one, but Grant Fuhr, Patrick Roy, and Ron Hextall will rank among the league's all-time great goalies. Even goaltenders became offensively minded. Ron Hextall scored two goals in the 1980s, one in the regular season and one in the playoffs. Grant Fuhr, who set a record by playing 75 games in the 1987-88 season, assisted on 14 goals in 1983-84, collecting more points than at least a dozen position players who played 50 games.

Of course, the record book is not etched in stone; it is compiled to be changed. As the game grows, records will continue to fall in the 1990s and beyond.

Questions

1. Who was the first player in NHL history to record at least 50 assists in ten consecutive seasons?
2. Four players hold the record for most penalty-shot goals in one season with two. However, one of these players actually scored three times. Can you name the player who had his third goal disallowed and the circumstances that resulted in the goal being called back?
3. This NHL All-Star was also the youngest man to ever coach in the Ontario Hockey League (OHL). Who was he and when did he have his stay behind the bench?
4. Who are the five defencemen who put their names in the record book by scoring at least 30 goals in a season during the 1980s?

5. The first player to score 50 goals in a season with two different teams notched his second 50-goal campaign in 1979-80. Name the player and the two clubs involved.

6. Name the six players who scored their 500th career goals during the 1980s.

7. In the 1980s, both Wayne Gretzky and Mike Bossy scored 50 goals in 50 games. The official NHL mark is based on the number of games played by the team, not on the number of games played by the individual. If the individual criteria was used, one more player would be added to that list. Who is he and when did he accomplish this unheralded feat?

8. Name the two players who set an NHL record for most points in one road game and accomplished this feat in the same game.

9. The Vancouver Canucks became the first team to score two penalty-shot goals in a game in 1982. Name the two shooters and the goaltender.

10. Which goaltender led the NHL in shutouts during the 1980s and how many zeroes did he post?

11. Five NHL teams won at least 400 games during the 1980s. Name those five clubs.

12. Which team recorded the fewest wins during the decade? How many wins did it record?

13. The Winnipeg Jets set a 1980s record for the greatest single-season improvement from one year to the next. By how many points did the team improve and who was the coach who led the charge?

14. Who was the first American-born player to record five goals in a game, and who were the victims of this feat?

15. Name the well-travelled veteran who played with six different teams between 1979-80 and 1988-89.

16. Who was the last man to go directly from being an active player to being the head coach of the same NHL team?

17. Who was the first man in NHL history to coach in four different decades?

18. The 1973-74 Los Angeles Kings' roster featured six players who went on to be coaches in the 1980s. Can you name the six teammates who would later be head coaches in the NHL?

19. Who was the youngest player ever to win the Hart Trophy as the NHL's MVP?

20. Who was the youngest defenceman in NHL history to score 30 goals in a season?

21. Who was the youngest captain in NHL history?

22. Who was the youngest player in NHL history to score 100 points in a season?

23. Who is the youngest player in NHL history to score 50 goals in a season?

24. During the 1950s, many talented hockey players dwelled in the minor leagues, surviving on a combination of brawn and brain. Four players who were members of the minor pro Winnipeg Warriors in 1955-56 and 1956-57 went on to serve as NHL executives in the 1980s. Name these four players and their jobs in the NHL.

25. Who was the youngest coach in NHL history?
26. Who was the first NHL coach to wear a beard?
27. Who was the only coach in NHL history to win at least 40 games each of his first three seasons?
28. Name the veteran who set a record by playing with 14 different pro teams in the 1980s.
29. Who was the youngest GM in NHL History?
30. In 1983-84, this member of the Toronto Maple Leafs became the first player in team history to score two penalty-shot goals in one season. Who is he?
31. Who set an NHL record for forwards by playing his first 69 games of the season without scoring a goal?
32. Who holds the NHL record for most shorthanded goals in a season by a defenceman?
33. Who was the only player in the 1980s to skate with four different NHL teams in one season?
34. The Edmonton Oilers are the only team to score 400 goals in a season, reaching that mark four times in the 1980s. Name the team that scored the second largest number of goals in one season.
35. Which team holds the record for worst penalty-killing percentage (67.7) for a season in NHL history?
36. Who holds the NHL record for most hat tricks in one playoff year?
37. Who holds the NHL record for consecutive games played?
38. Which two players set an NHL record during the

1980s for the fastest goal from the start of a game?

39. Who was the first player in NHL history to score at least 50 goals in nine consecutive years?

40. Name the players who combined to score the two fastest shorthanded goals in NHL history.

Answers

1. Bernie Federko, the St. Louis Blues' all-time leading scorer, was the first NHL player to compile at least 50 assists in ten straight seasons, from 1978-79 to 1987-88.

2. Joe Mullen is tied with Pat Egan, Greg Terrion, and Mike Gartner with two penalty-shot goals in a season. Mullen actually scored a third goal in a game on March 28th, 1987, on Los Angeles goaltender Al Jensen. After the goal was scored, Kings coach Mike Murphy called for a stick measurement. Referee Kerry Fraser ruled that Mullen used an illegal stick and disallowed the goal.

3. Seventeen-year-old Brian Bellows guided the Kitchener Rangers for two games during the 1981-82 season when coach Joe Crozier was suspended.

4. Paul Coffey (four times), Denis Potvin (1979-80), Raymond Bourque (1983-84), Phil Housley (1983-84), and Doug Wilson (1981-82) all scored at least 30 goals from their positions on the blueline.

5. Pierre Larouche, who became the first player to score 50 goals in the history of the Pittsburgh Penguins franchise in 1976, scored his 50th goal for the Montreal Canadiens in an 8-4 win over Chicago on March 25, 1980.

6. Marcel Dionne (1982), Guy Lafleur (1983), Mike Bossy (1986), Gilbert Perreault (1986), Wayne Gretzky (1986), and Lanny McDonald (1989) all reached the 500-goal mark in the 1980s.

7. Jari Kurri scored 50 goals in his first 50 games played during the 1984-85 season. Kurri's goal, scored in the team's 53rd game, came on February 3 against Hartford's Greg Millen.

8. Peter and Anton Stastny each collected eight points in Quebec's 11-7 victory over Washington on February 22, 1981.

9. Thomas Gradin and Ivan Hlinka both slipped penalty-shot pucks past Detroit Red Wing goaltender Gilles Gilbert on February 11, 1982.

10. Mike Liut, who patrolled the crease for St. Louis and Hartford in the 1980s, recorded 20 shutouts during the decade, one more than Pete Peeters of the Flyers, Bruins, and Capitals.

11. Edmonton (446), Philadelphia (446), Montreal (435), Boston (418), and the NY Islanders (414) all recorded 400 wins in the decade.

12. The New Jersey Devils had the poorest record in the 1980s, winning 237 games, losing 466 times and tying 97 for a winning percentage of .357. The once-proud Toronto Maple Leafs were the next-worse team with a winning percentage of .388.

13. In 1980-81, the Jets compiled a 9-57-14 record. The following season, with former University of Toronto coach Tom Watt behind the bench, the Jets improved by 48 points, posting a 33-33-14 record to climb from fifth to second in the Norris Division.

14. Mark Pavelich scored five times on Hartford Whalers goaltender Greg Millen in the Rangers' 11-3 victory on February 23, 1983. He was only the second NY Ranger to accomplish the feat.

15. During the 1980s, Brent Ashton kept his hockey equipment bag packed. He played with Vancouver (1979-81), Colorado/New Jersey (1981-83), Minnesota (1983-85), Quebec (1985-1987), Detroit (1987-88), and Winnipeg (1988-89). In 1982 Ashton was sent to the Jets as compensation for Vancouver's signing of Ivan Hlinka, but he was quickly dispatched to Colorado before ever suiting up for Winnipeg.

16. Brian Sutter became the St. Louis Blues coach in June 1988 after 12 seasons as a player for the Blues.

17. Punch Imlach coached from 1959 through 1969 for Toronto, 1970 through 1977 for Buffalo, and then with Toronto again in 1979-80.

18. The success of the 1973-74 Los Angeles Kings can be equated to not only the brain power of Bob Pulford but to that of six future NHL coaches. On offence the Kings had Mike Murphy, Dan Maloney, Butch Goring, and Bob Berry. Back on the blue line were Bob Murdoch and Barry Long.

19. Wayne Gretzky was 19 years, five months old when he captured the Hart Trophy as the league MVP in June 1980.
20. Phil Housley turned 20 on March 9, 1984, the season he scored 30 goals for Buffalo in just his second year in the NHL.
21. Brian Bellows was just 19 years, one month old when he was named captain with Minnesota in 1983-84.
22. Dale Hawerchuk scored his 100th point a month shy of his 19th birthday in March 1982, with Winnipeg. He finished that season with a total of 103 points and won the Calder Trophy as the league's rookie of the year.
23. Wayne Gretzky scored his 50th goal of the 1979-80 season (his first in the NHL) at age 19 years, 2 months.
24. The 1955-56 championship Winnipeg Warriors featured two future NHL coaches, Fred Shero and Mike Nykoluk. One year later, Nykoluk departed the Warriors and Shero was joined by two rookie goaltenders – Gerry McNamara and Eddie Johnston. McNamara and Johnston would later make their mark in the NHL as, respectively, a general manager and a GM/coach. Shero coached the Flyers and Rangers. Nykoluk had a brief coaching stint with the Leafs after years as an assistant in New York.
25. Michel Bergeron was 25 years, 11 months old when he became coach of the Quebec Nordiques on October 20, 1980.

26. Larry Pleau, who coached the Hartford Whalers in 1980-81, was the first NHL coach to wear a beard.
27. Mike Keenan won 53 games in both 1984-85 and 1985-86 and 46 games in 1986-87 as the head coach of the Philadelphia Flyers.
28. Jeff Brubaker played for seven NHL teams, one International Hockey League (IHL) team, one Central Hockey League (CHL) team, and five American Hockey League (AHL) teams.
29. Gord Stellick was 30 years old when he was named GM of the Toronto Maple Leafs on April 28, 1988.
30. Greg Terrion scored both penalty-shot goals while playing for Toronto in 1983-84. The first came against Chicago's Tony Esposito on October 15 in a 10-8 Leafs win and the second came against Chicago's Murray Bannerman on January 14 in a 2-2 tie.
31. Billy Carroll, a forward with the New York Islanders, played the first 69 games of the 1982-83 season before scoring a goal.
32. Paul Coffey had nine shorthanded goals with Edmonton in 1985-86.
33. Dennis O'Brien played for Minnesota, Colorado, Cleveland, and Boston during the 1979-80 season.
34. The Calgary Flames scored 397 goals during the 1987-88 season, 34 more than the Oilers.
35. In 1979-80 the Los Angeles Kings allowed 94 powerplay goals in 291 opposition attempts for a penalty-killing percentage of 67.7%, the lowest in

NHL history. Interestingly, the Kings also had the second-best powerplay in the NHL, scoring on 26.7% of their manpower advantages.

36. Jari Kurri of the Oilers set the mark with four in 1984-85. He had a four-goal game, and three three-goal games.

37. Doug Jarvis played in 964 consecutive games with Montreal, Washington, and Hartford from October 1975 through October 1987. He played his entire NHL career -- 12-plus seasons – without missing a game.

38. Winnipeg's Doug Smail and the Islanders' Bryan Trottier share the NHL record for fastest goal from the start of a game. Both scored just five seconds after the opening faceoff.

39. The New York Islanders' Mike Bossy scored at least 50 goals in nine consecutive seasons, from 1977-78 to 1985-86.

40. Calgary's Doug Gilmour and Paul Ranheim set an NHL record for the fastest two shorthanded goals, scoring just four seconds apart. The pair of tallies came in an 8-8 tie against the Nordiques on October 17, 1989.

Disc Johnnies

Each of the players pictured below has the same first name. Can you identify the players? Answers on page 133.

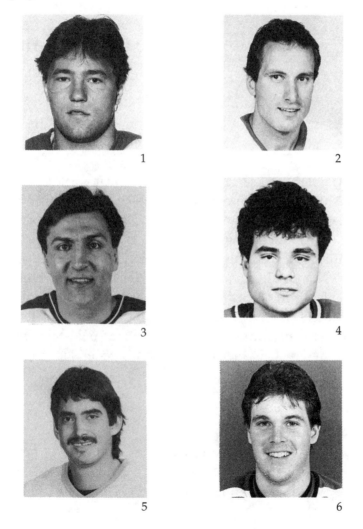

1

2

3

4

5

6

2

The Champions

FOR THE FIRST TIME IN A DECADE SINCE THE 1940s, four different teams won the Stanley Cup in the 1980s, with the Edmonton Oilers and the New York Islanders combining to win eight championships. Interrupting their combined dynasties were the Montreal Canadiens, who won their 23rd championship in 1986, and the Calgary Flames, first-time winners in 1989. The Flames, who shifted from Atlanta to Alberta in 1980, were painstakingly molded by Cliff Fletcher, the team's general manager since 1972. Although the Flames had reached the playoffs in seventeen of their first eighteen seasons, it wasn't until 1989 that they were able to close out a season in Stanley Cup style.

The decade began with the launch of a new dynasty. The New York Islanders won four consecutive Stanley Cup titles from 1980 to 1983. Bill Torrey, the organizational genius who built the Islanders, did so by studying both the managerial techniques of Montreal's mastermind, Sam Pollock, and the mistakes of other expansion teams, like the California Seals, who had given the bow-tied Torrey his first NHL appointment. Torrey fiercely protected his draft selections, rarely trading a pick away unless it would provide optimum return. Of the 31 players who played for the Islanders in the 1979-80 season, 23 were acquired through the draft. The nucleus of the team remained intact through their four-year reign as Stanley Cup champions, with only peripheral reconstruction taking place. In the Islanders' four-year term in the Stanley Cup office, sixteen players appeared on all four championship clubs.

The Edmonton Oilers won their first Stanley Cup in only their fifth NHL campaign, in 1983-84. While, like the Islanders, their main cast of players remained consistent, general manager Glen Sather was constantly changing the supporting players, bringing in a wide array of role players, such as Kent Nilsson, Reijo Ruotsalainen, Moe Lemay, Larry Melnyk, Dave Hannan, and Mark Napier. Most of these players were NHL veterans, additionally motivated by the opportunity to finally capture a Stanley Cup ring, an honour that escaped Sather throughout his eleven-year NHL career as a journeyman left-winger.

The nucleus of those championship Oiler teams started with Wayne Gretzky, one of only two Oilers from the WHA club to win the Cup. The remaining base of talent – Fuhr, Messier, Anderson, Kurri, Lowe,

Huddy – were all obtained through the entry draft. Interestingly, these seven players were present on all four Stanley Cup-winning teams.

The Montreal Canadiens won their lone Cup of the 1980s with a roster of youngsters (Patrick Roy, Claude Lemieux, David Maley, Kjell Dahlin, Petr Svoboda, Chris Chelios) and veterans (Guy Carbonneau, Bob Gainey, Larry Robinson, Bobby Smith, Ryan Walter, Rick Green). However, by the end of the decade, the majority of these players would be retired or serving in other organizations as the Habs would be rebuilding again.

The mainstays of the Calgary club – Rob Ramage, Lanny McDonald, Tim Hunter, Brad McCrimmon, Ric Nattress, and Doug Gilmour – had all been obtained through the trade market. Fletcher cleverly mixed these veterans with draft selections like Joe Nieuwendyk, Mike Vernon, Theo Fleury, and Gary Roberts to arrive with a winning combination.

The 1980s marked the first time since the NHL's earliest days that three teams who had never won a Cup were crowned as champions. It was a decade of exceptional performances that ushered in a new era of hockey, a period that has continued to thrive in the 1990s.

Questions

1. Who was the only rookie coach to win the Stanley Cup in the 1980s and in which year did he lead his team to victory?

2. This player was the first player in NHL history to score the Cup-winning goal in back-to-back seasons. Can you name this opportunistic marksman?
3. This defenceman became only the second player in league history to score a powerplay goal in overtime during the Stanley Cup finals. Who was the player and who was the goaltender who allowed the timely tally?
4. Who is the only player to win an Olympic gold medal and a Stanley Cup ring in the same season?
5. Only two players who appeared on an WHA championship team in the 1970s played on a Stanley Cup-winning team in the 1980s. Name the two players and the teams they were with when they captured their titles.
6. Name the player who holds the NHL record for consecutive playoff appearances without ever winning the Stanley Cup.
7. Who was the first player to record six assists in a playoff game?
8. Of the 32 players who appeared with the Stanley Cup champion New York Islanders in 1979-80, only five were obtained through trades. Can you name the "acquired" quintet?
9. Name the two players who set an NHL record by scoring three shorthanded goals in the same series.
10. There were four overtime goals scored in the Stanley Cup finals in the 1980s. Can you name the quartet of extra-session heroes?
11. Who scored the most playoff overtime goals in the 1980s and who did he score the goals against?

12. Name the only player to make his NHL debut in the Stanley Cup finals during the 1980s.

13. Who was the only player in the 1980s to score five goals in a playoff game?

14. Tim Kerr wrote his name into the NHL record books on April 13, 1985. Which offensive feat did Kerr turn that no other NHLer has been able to match?

15. Which team registered the most shots on goal in a Stanley Cup final game during the 1980s? Which team registered the fewest?

16. Who was first defenceman in NHL history to score two career playoff hat tricks?

17. In 1981, this New York Ranger became only the second player in NHL history to score a goal on a penalty-shot during the playoffs. Who was he?

18. Who set an NHL record in 1988-89 for most power play goals in a playoff series?

19. In the 1980s, two goaltenders allowed six post-season hat-tricks to be scored against each of them. Who were they?

20. Which team holds the NHL playoff record of 13 goals in one game?

21. Name the rookie who set an NHL record for the fastest two goals from the start of a period in a playoff game.

22. Who is the only defenceman in NHL playoff history to score three career overtime goals?

23. Who scored the last Stanley Cup-winning goal that came in overtime?

24. Which Hall of Famer won his only Stanley Cup in the final game of his 16-year NHL career?

25. Who holds the record for most points by a defenceman in a single playoff game? Also, name the opposing team.

26. Who is the youngest player to win the Conn Smythe Trophy?

27. Who holds the NHL record for most points in a playoff year by a rookie and how many points did the youngster compile?

28. On May 25, 1989, the Calgary Flames defeated the Montreal Canadiens 4-2 to win the Stanley Cup championship. It was the first time since 1928 that a Montreal team had lost the final game of the championship finals on home ice. Name the visiting team that won the Stanley Cup on Forum ice in the 1928 finals.

29. Who holds the Stanley Cup playoff record for the fastest overtime goal?

30. Who scored the Stanley Cup-winning goal for the Montreal Canadiens in 1986?

31. When the Vancouver Canucks reached the 1982 Stanley Cup finals, they became the third Vancouver team to appear in the championship round. Name the first two Vancouver teams to play for the Stanley Cup prior to the 1980s.

32. Two teams in the 1980s won eight straight road games in the playoffs. Who were the teams and in which years did they have their travelling success?

33. Who was the only goaltender in the 1980s to win an AHL championship and the Stanley Cup in back-to-back seasons?
34. Who was the only Toronto Maple Leaf player to register a playoff hat-trick in the 1980s?
35. Who was the only player to record a playoff hat-trick for two different teams in the 1980s?
36. Name the player who appeared in the Stanley Cup finals with three different teams during the 1980s. Also, name the teams.
37. In the 1986 playoffs, two players who didn't reach the finals tied for the lead in post-season scoring. Who were they?
38. Who was the only defenceman to lead all post-season scorers in the 1980s?
39. Who was the only player in the 1980s to score three goals in one period during the Stanley Cup finals?
40. Name the only sub-.500 team to make it all the way to the Stanley Cup finals during the 1980s. What was the club's regular-season record?

Answers

1. Jean Perron was the freshman coach who piloted the Montreal Canadiens to the Stanley Cup in 1986. He was the first rookie coach since the Canadiens' Al MacNeil in 1971 to win the championship in his first season behind the bench.
2. Mike Bossy scored the Cup winner in both 1982

and 1983 for the New York Islanders. In 1982, his goal eliminated the Vancouver Canucks, while in 1983, he ousted the Edmonton Oilers with a goal at 12:39 of the first period. In the 1983 Wales Conference finals against Boston, Bossy scored all four winning goals in the Islanders' six-game victory.

3. Denis Potvin became the first player since Bill Cook in 1933 to score a powerplay goal in overtime during the finals. Potvin's goal, which gave the New York Islanders their first victory in the Stanley Cup finals, was scored against Pete Peeters of the Philadelphia Flyers.

4. Ken Morrow, who was key member of the U.S. Olympic Team's "Miracle on Ice" in Lake Placid, joined the New York Islanders after the Games and was a member of the 1980 Stanley Cup champions.

5. Kent Nilsson was on the Avco Cup-winning Winnipeg Jets in 1979 and the 1987 Stanley Cup champion Edmonton Oilers. Willy Lindstrom was a member of the WHA champion Jets in 1978 and 1979 and the NHL champion Oilers in 1984 and 1985.

6. Brad Park, who never missed the playoffs in his 17-year career with the New York Rangers, Boston Bruins, and Detroit Red Wings, was never on a championship team.

7. Mikko Leinonen recorded six assists for the New York Rangers in their 7-3 victory over the Philadelphia Flyers on April 8, 1982. These

proved to be the only six assists Leinonen recorded in the playoffs that season.

8. Wayne Merrick, Gord Lane, Bob Bourne, Butch Goring, and Chico Resch were all acquired through trades prior to the Isles winning their first Stanley Cup.

9. Bill Barber scored a trio of shorthanded goals against the Minnesota North Stars in the 1980 semi-finals. Wayne Presley of the Blackhawks matched Barber's mark against Detroit in the 1989 divisional semi-finals.

10. Bob Nystrom (game six vs. Philadelphia in 1980), Brian Skrudland (game two vs. Calgary in 1986), Jari Kurri (game two vs. Philadelphia in 1987), and Ryan Walter (game four vs. Calgary, 1989) were the overtime heroes.

11. Dale Hunter of the Nordiques and Capitals scored overtime goals against Philadelphia (April 12, 1981), Montreal (April 13, 1982, April 23, 1985), and Philadelphia (April 16, 1988) in the 1980s.

12. Esa Tikkanen made his NHL debut with the Edmonton Oilers in game one of the Stanley Cup finals against the Philadelphia Flyers. Tikkanen played three games and earned the right to have his name inscribed on the Stanley Cup.

13. Mario Lemieux fired five goals past Ron Hextall and Ken Wregget in Pittsburgh's 10-7 victory over the Flyers in game five of the division finals on April 25, 1989.

14. Kerr scored three powerplay goals in the second

period of the Philadelphia Flyers' 6-5 win over the New York Rangers in the Patrick Division semi-finals.

15. The Edmonton Oilers recorded 43 shots against the Philadelphia Flyers in game seven of the 1987 finals. The Boston Bruins, with 12 shots in game two of the 1988 championship series, had the fewest shots of the decade.

16. Paul Reinhart of the Calgary Flames was the first defenceman to record two hat tricks in the play-offs. The first came in 1983 in the Smythe Division finals against Edmonton and the second came in the 1984 Smythe Division semi-finals against Vancouver.

17. Anders Hedberg of the Rangers became the second player to score on a penalty-shot in the play-offs when he beat the Blues' Mike Liut on April 17, 1981, in a 6-4 Rangers win. The first was Minnesota's Wayne Connelly, who beat the Kings' Terry Sawchuk in a 7-5 Minnesota win on April 9, 1968.

18. Chris Kontos scored six powerplay goals for Los Angeles in the 1989 playoffs against Edmonton.

19. Murray Bannerman and Pete Peeters partici-pated in six three-or-more-goal games during the 1980s. Bannerman allowed three of Jari Kurri's hat-tricks in 1985 while Peeters surrendered two of Mike Bossy's "tricks" in 1983.

20. The Edmonton Oilers whipped 13 pucks past Los Angeles goaltenders in the Oilers' 13-3 thrashing of the Kings on April 9, 1987.

21. Pat LaFontaine, who joined the New York Islanders after the 1984 Olympics, scored two goals in the first 35 seconds of the third period of a game against the Edmonton Oilers on May 19, 1984.

22. Ken Morrow scored three overtime goals during his playoff career with the New York Islanders.

23. Bobby Nystrom scored the Cup winner in over-time for the Islanders on May 24, 1980, to give them a 5-4 win over Philadelphia.

24. Lanny McDonald won the Stanley Cup with Calgary in 1989 after 16 NHL seasons with Toronto, Colorado, and the Flames.

25. The Edmonton Oilers' Paul Coffey set a playoff record with six points during a 10-5 Edmonton win over Chicago at Northlands Coliseum on May 14, 1985.

26. Patrick Roy of Montreal first won the Smythe Trophy as the playoff MVP in 1986 at the age of 20.

27. Dino Ciccarelli, who joined the Minnesota North Stars for the final 32 games of the 1980-81 season, recorded a rookie record 21 points in 19 playoff games in his first taste of post-season play.

28. On April 14, 1928, the New York Rangers defeated the Montreal Maroons 2-1 to capture the franchise's first Stanley Cup title.

29. Brian Skrudland scored at :09 of overtime in game two of the 1986 finals to give Montreal a 3-2 win at Calgary on May 18, 1986.

30. Bobby Smith scored at 10:30 of the third period of

game five of the 1986 finals to seal Montreal's 4-3 victory and bring the Habs their 23rd Stanley Cup title.

31. The Vancouver Maroons of the WCHL lost the Cup final in 1923 and 1924 while the Vancouver Millionaires lost to the Toronto St. Pats in 1922.

32. The New York Islanders won eight consecutive games on the road in 1980, while the Philadelphia Flyers captured eight straight games away from home during their Stanley Cup run in 1987.

33. Patrick Roy won the Calder Cup with the Sherbrooke Jets in 1984-85 and captured the Stanley Cup with the Montreal Canadiens in 1985-86.

34. Ed Olczyk scored three goals against Detroit in the Leafs' 6-5 victory on April 12, 1988.

35. Peter Zezel fired three goals for Philadelphia in the Flyers' 7-1 win over the New York Rangers in 1986 and scored a hat-trick for St. Louis in the Blues' 6-1 win over Minnesota in 1989.

36. Ken Linseman went to the championship round with Philadelphia (1980), Edmonton (1983-84), and Boston (1988). He won his only Cup title with the Oilers in 1984.

37. St. Louis Blues' Doug Gilmour and Bernie Federko each compiled 21 points to tie for the lead in post-season scoring.

38. Al MacInnis led all scorers in the 1989 playoffs with seven goals and 24 assists.

39. Wayne Gretzky notched a hat-trick in the first period of game three of the 1987 finals between Edmonton and Philadelphia.

40. The Vancouver Canucks, who registered a 30-33-17 record during the 1981-82 season, defeated Calgary, Los Angeles, and Chicago to make it to the championship final.

Lord Stanley's Men

Listed below are some seasons and the teams which won the Stanley Cup during each of those seasons. Under each season is listed four players who played for the winner. Two of the players listed were either traded during the year or played 10 games or less during the regular schedule and thus were ineligible to have their names engraved on the Stanley Cup. Circle the two players whose names do appear on the Stanley Cup for the season indicated. Answers on page 133.

1980-81, New York Islanders
Roland Melanson, Chico Resch, Duane Sutter, Brent Sutter

1983-84, Edmonton Oilers
Esa Tikkanen, Marc Habschied, Randy Gregg, Charlie Huddy

1985-86, Montreal Canadiens
Shayne Corson, Alfie Turcotte, Mike Lalor, Mario Tremblay

1988-89, Calgary Flames
Hakan Loob, Mark Hunter, Paul Ranheim, Stu Grimson

3

Rookies of Renown

PERHAPS NO DECADE IN THE HISTORY OF THE NHL has seen a wider variety of new talent enter the league than the 1980s. With the NHL opening its doors to Europe and the American college system, players who were never considered as NHL prospects were now given the opportunity to excel, and many of them jumped at the chance.

Of all the rookies who joined the NHL family in the 1980s (excluding Wayne Gretzky, who was not considered a rookie because of his professional experience in the WHA), a quartet of names stands above the others. Dale Hawerchuk, the Winnipeg Jets' first selection and the first player chosen overall in the 1981 Entry Draft, resurrected a team that had finished last overall in the 1980-81 season. The Jets climbed from nine wins and 32 points to 33 wins and 80 points in Hawerchuk's initial campaign. Although the Jets never reached the Stanley Cup winner's circle,

Hawerchuk became the team's all-time leading scorer, establishing thirteen individual club records by averaging 100 points a season through his first eight NHL seasons.

The Pittsburgh Penguins emerged from a decade-long deep freeze, thanks to the efforts of Mario Lemieux, one of the greatest performers to ever play the game. Lemieux's ability to score goals with two defencemen draped all over him is only a minute component of his game. He is an exceptional passer, a diligent forechecker, and a crafty competitor. Lemieux's performance during the 1987 Canada Cup, when he teamed with Wayne Gretzky, was not only a highlight of the decade, but a benchmark in the history of the game.

Paul Coffey, perhaps hockey's most gifted skater since Bobby Orr, rewrote the defenceman's record book during the 1980s, reaching the 100-point plateau on four occasions. In 1985-86, Coffey fired 48 goals to join the Orr as the only defenceman in the history of the league to reach the 40-goal milestone. Coffey's offensive exploits often overshadowed his defensive abilities, but he was a reliable rearguard, whose speed often enabled him to get back into position after an offensive foray.

The European influence on the 1980s is best exemplified by Jari Kurri. Although Peter Stastny had finer offensive numbers, Kurri's ability to perform under playoff pressure when checking is tight made him the decade's top offensive player. In the four years the Oilers won the Stanley Cup, Kurri led all playoff goal-scorers, providing the Oilers with a fourth highly skilled marksman capable of scoring quickly if opponents focused only on Gretzky, Messier, or Anderson.

Other notable rookies include Denis Savard, who never finished lower than second in Blackhawk team scoring throughout the decade; Ray Bourque, an All-Star in each of his ten seasons in the 1980s, and Steve Yzerman, who rewrote much of the Detroit Red Wings' record book.

As well, players from the American college system, such as Kevin Stevens, Chris Chelios, John Cullen, Brian Leetch, and Jon Casey, made considerable contributions to their teams and to the league during the decade. As the 1980s came to a close, another door was opened when arrangements were made with the Soviet hockey federation to have their players finally compete in the NHL. The 1990s saw a flood of Soviet talent, including names such as Makarov, Fetisov, Krutov, and Larionov. With a talent base that now embraces the earth, the NHL can truly be considered the world's first global league.

Questions

1. The NHL has been selecting an All-Rookie Team since 1982-83. Who were the members of the first all-freshman squad?
2. Who compiled the most points in his rookie season yet did not win the Calder Trophy?

3. Name the only rookie defenceman to record six assists in a game.
4. Who was the leading scorer among rookies in the 1979-80 season?
5. This defenceman, who has played for four teams during his NHL career, set a record for assists by a rookie rearguard. Who is he and how many assists did he collect in his freshman campaign?
6. In the 1980s, four rookies jumped directly to the NHL from high school. Name the fast-rising newcomers.
7. Name the only rookie to graduate to the NHL from American college hockey after starting his career in Canadian Major Junior?
8. Two rookies who made their debut in the NHL during the 1980s actually returned to junior after spending an entire season in the NHL. Name these returning rookies.
9. Who was the first Soviet-trained athlete to play in the NHL with the permission of the Soviet Hockey Federation?
10. Who was the first rookie in the 1980s to jump from Canadian university hockey directly to the NHL without spending any time in the minors?
11. Name the NHLer who was the first Hobey Baker Award winner as the NCAA college player of the year.
12. Who was the first rookie in the 1980s to win a major award other than the Calder Trophy in his first season and which award he did receive?

13. Name the only rookie to score 50 goals in his first season during the 1980s.
14. Only one rookie defenceman in the 1980s managed to score 20 goals in his freshman season. Name him.
15. This player tied a 36-year-old mark by scoring three goals in his first NHL game. Who was the marksmen who opened his NHL career with a hat-trick?
16. Who was the first player in NHL history to score 100 points in his rookie season?
17. Who was the second NHL player to score 100 points in his rookie season?
18. Which rookie began his NHL career in the 1980s with 13 goals in his first 15 games?
19. Name the only rookie to record two hat-tricks in 1985-86.
20. Name the only player to win IHL rookie-of-the-year honours before winning the Calder Trophy.
21. Who holds the NHL record for most penalty minutes by a rookie goalie and how many minutes of "sin-bin" time did he accumulate?
22. Who holds the NHL record for most penalty minutes in a season by a rookie?
23. Which NHL player wore uniform #98 during his rookie season?
24. Who was the first rookie in the 1980s to score his first NHL goal on a penalty shot?
25. Name this future NHL referee who as a player received 29 minutes in penalties in his first NHL game with the Quebec Nordiques.

26. Who was the last Sutter brother to score his first NHL goal?

27. Only one winner of the Calder Trophy during the 1980s played in the AHL before becoming an NHL regular. Who was he?

28. Name the Boston rookie who tied a team record with seven points in one game during the 1981-82 season.

29. Who was the first rookie in New Jersey Devils' history to record a hat-trick?

30. Name the Pittsburgh Penguins rookie who scored on the first three shots he took in the NHL.

31. A rookie goaltender, with only two games of NHL experience, led the Boston Bruins to an upset series win over Buffalo in the 1982 playoffs before losing in seven games to Quebec. Who was the reliable rookie?

32. In 1983, a promising Boston rookie's career came to an end when he suffered a brain hemorrhage. Do you know this unfortunate freshman's name?

33. Who holds the record for most points in a season by a rookie left winger?

34. During the 1980s, only two of the ten prospects selected first overall in the entry draft have won the Calder Trophy as the rookie of the year. Who were they?

35. Name the only Calder Trophy winner to serve as a head coach in the NHL during the 1980s.

Answers

1. The members of the NHL's first All-Rookie Team were Pelle Lindbergh (goal), Scott Stevens and Phil Housley (defence), Dan Daoust (centre), Steve Larmer (right wing), and Mats Naslund (left wing).
2. Neal Broten, who joined the Minnesota North Stars in 1981-82, compiled 98 points but lost rookie-of-the-year honours to Dale Hawerchuk.
3. Calgary's Gary Suter recorded six assists on April 4, 1986, in the Flames' 9-3 win over the Edmonton Oilers.
4. Mike Foligno compiled 71 points in 1979-80 to lead all rookie scorers. Wayne Gretzky – then in his first NHL season – was not considered a rookie because he had played in the WHA.
5. Larry Murphy, who has played with Los Angeles, Washington, Minnesota, and Pittsburgh, collected a rookie record 60 assists in 1980-81.
6. Phil Housley (1982-83), Bob Carpenter (1981-82), Tom Barrasso (1983-84), and Brian Lawton (1983-84) all moved directly from high school hockey to the NHL.
7. Troy Murray made his NHL debut with the Chicago Blackhawks in 1981-82 directly from the University of North Dakota. Murray had played major junior hockey with the Lethbridge Broncos of the WHL in 1979-80.
8. Sylvain Cote spent the entire 1985-86 season with

the Hartford Whalers, but returned to the Hull Olympiques of the Quebec Major Junior Hockey League (QMJHL) in 1985-86. Joe Cirella played 65 games with the Colorado Rockies in 1981-82, but returned to junior with the Oshawa Generals in 1982-83.

9. Sergei Priakin, a 26-year-old right winger from the Soviet Wings, made his debut with the Calgary Flames in April 1989, appearing in two regular-season and one playoff game for the Flames.

10. Mike Ridley, the Canadian University Player of the Year with the University of Manitoba in 1984, made his debut with the New York Rangers in 1985-86, playing in all 80 games and leading the team in scoring with 22 goals and 43 assists.

11. Neal Broten, who was the first Hobey Baker winner in 1981, was called up to the North Stars at the end of the 1980-81 season and scored two goals in his first three NHL games.

12. Tom Barrasso of the Buffalo Sabres won the Vezina Trophy in addition to the Calder Trophy in his inaugural NHL campaign.

13. Joe Nieuwendyk fired 51 pucks past opposition goaltenders in his initial NHL season with the Calgary Flames in 1987-88

14. Brian Leetch scored 22 goals from his blueline position for the New York Rangers in 1988-89.

15. Real "Buddy" Cloutier scored three goals for the Quebec Nordiques in his – and the team's – first NHL game.

16. Quebec's Peter Stastny picked up an assist on a Michel Goulet goal in a 4-0 win over Montreal on March 28, 1981, to become the first rookie to score 100 points in a season. He finished the year with 39 goals and 70 assists for 109 points.

17. Dale Hawerchuk had 45 goals and 58 assists for 103 points for Winnipeg in 1981-82 and won the Calder Trophy as the league's rookie of the year.

18. Pat LaFontaine of the New York Islanders scored 13 goals in his first 15 games, which were the last 15 games of the Islanders' 1983-84 schedule.

19. Detroit's Petr Klima recored two three-goal games for the Red Wings in 1985-86.

20. Ed Belfour captured IHL's top rookie award in 1987-88 and the Calder Trophy in 1990-91.

21. Philadelphia's rookie goalie Ron Hextall set an NHL record with 104 PIM in 1986-87, his first with the Flyers.

22. Detroit's Joey Kocur set an NHL record for freshmen with 377 PIM with the Red Wings in 1985-86.

23. Brian Lawton wore #98 with Minnesota in 1983-84.

24. Philadelphia's Ilkka Sinisalo became the third player in league history to score his first NHL goal on a penalty shot on October 11, 1981. Sinisalo beat Paul Harrison as the Flyers beat Pittsburgh, 8-2.

25. Quebec rookie and future referee Paul Stewart fought Boston's Terry O'Reilly, Stan Jonathan, and Al Secord in his first NHL game on November 27, 1979.

26. On October 23, 1983, rookie Rich Sutter scored a goal in his first NHL game. He became the sixth Sutter brother to score a goal in the NHL.

27. Steve Larmer played 74 games with the AHL's New Brunswick Hawks in 1981-82 before winning the rookie of the year award with Chicago in 1982-83.

28. On April 4, 1982, Boston's Barry Pederson scored three goals and added four assists for seven points in a 7-2 Bruins' win over Hartford. The seven points established a team record for most points by a rookie.

29. On Halloween Night, 1984, Uli Hiemer became the first Devils defenceman and also the first Devils rookie to record a hat-trick, although New Jersey lost 7-6 to Pittsburgh.

30. Rob Brown, who debuted with the Penguins on October 21, 1987.

31. Mike Moffat appeared in all 11 playoff games the Bruins played in 1982. These would prove to be the only NHL playoff games of his career.

32. Normand Leveille, who had compiled nine points in nine games during the 1982-83 season, suffered a brain hemorrhage in between periods of a Bruins-Canucks game and was unable to play hockey again.

33. In 1980-81, the Quebec Nordiques' Anton Stastny recorded 85 points to set a rookie mark for points by a freshman left-winger.

34. Winnipeg's first pick in 1981, Dale Hawerchuk of Cornwall, won the Calder Trophy in 1982 and

Mario Lemieux, Pittsburgh's number-one choice in 1984, was top rookie in 1985.

35. Bernie Geoffrion, the Calder Trophy winner for the Montreal Canadiens in 1952, coached the Montreal Canadiens for thirty games during the 1979-80 season.

Seasons in the Sun

Match the player on the left with the first season he played a game in the NHL. Answers on page 134.

Steve Larmer	1983-84
Chris Kontos	1980-81
Pelle Lindbergh	1984-85
Joel Otto	1982-83
Marty McSorley	1981-82
Bill Ranford	1985-86

Statistically Speaking

THE 1980s WERE A FACT-FINDER'S DREAM, OR NIGHT-mare, depending on your point of view. The refining of various statistical categories such as plus/minus rating, shooting percentage, game-winning, game-tying, and overtime goals gave the hockey historian greater in-depth information to compile, digest, and study than at any time in the history of the game. In hockey's formative years, even rudimentary information such as shots on goal and times of goals were difficult to determine. In newspaper summaries of the 1930s, goal times were judged on the time elapsed since the last goal was scored. For instance, a goal recorded as 8:13 meant that length of time had ticked off the clock since the preceding goal.

By the 1980s, every possible facet and permutation of the game was being painstakingly compiled and computed for all hockey historians and enthusiasts to enjoy and study. Today each player's ice time is recorded, the number of skaters on the ice registered when a goal is scored, a goaltender's ice time broken down to the second. Giveaways, takeaways, face-off efficiency, icings, hits, and unforced errors are all part of the statistical package that details the flow of the game. The 1978-79 *NHL Guide* carried only ten statistical categories in its synopsis of the 1977-78 season. By contrast, the 1988-89 *NHL Guide and Record Book* broke the 1987-88 season into fifty different statistical components, including fourteen team statistical categories (among them: team streaks, shorthanded goals for and against, overtime records) and fifteen rookie categories.

The arrival of the video age and the addition of assistant coaches, both on the bench and in the press box, made these previously obscure statistical categories simpler to compile and provided coaching staffs with an added perspective when preparing game charts for upcoming opponents.

The hockey pool reached unprecedented popularity in the 1980s, creating a new breed of hockey fan. Today there are dozens of books, stat sheets, magazines, fanzines, and data services to provide the undernourished hockey mathematician with up-to-the-minute numbers, figures, charts, and graphs. The success of hockey pools and fantasy leagues has compelled fans to scrutinize even the most obscure hockey information for added insight as to which players might have a "career" year, thereby carrying the would-be general manager to the winner's circle.

However, for the general fan, the most significant hockey data continues to be goals and assists – two categories dominated in the 1980s by players named Gretzky and Lemieux. Other notable performances of the 1980s included Grant Fuhr's record 75-game season and Billy Smith's mark for post-season games and minutes played, (132 playoff games comprising 7,645 minutes). Team-wise, the Philadelphia Flyers compiled a 35-game unbeaten streak in 1979-80, going almost three months without a loss.

For fans of hockey statistics, the 1980s represented nothing less than a revolution in the collection and organization of "hard" hockey information.

Questions

1. Which team set an NHL record for most games without a loss from the start of the season? When did it accomplish its record streak and how many games did it go before losing its first game?
2. Which NHL team's record for consecutive winning seasons was ended in 1983-84?
3. On March 14, 1983, this Calgary Flame defenceman had the distinction of scoring the National Hockey League's 100th penalty-shot goal. Name this player, the goaltender, and the team he scored against.
4. Who led all NHLers in regular-season games played in the 1980s?
5. Who played the most games in one season during the 1980s and how many games did he play?

6. Only two defencemen scored four goals in a game during the decade. Who were they and in which years did they have their four-goal games?

7. Who had the fewest penalty minutes of any top-ten scorer during the 1980s? How many penalty minutes did he record?

8. During the 1980s, which two players scored their 500th career goals into an empty net?

9. Who scored the most regular-season overtime goals during the 1980s and how many did he score?

10. Which team had the most 20-goal scorers in a single season during the 1980s? How many 20-goal men did they have?

11. Who was the all-time leading scorer among American-born players when the 1980s came to a close?

12. Which team won the most overtime games during the 1980s?

13. This team set an NHL record for most powerplay goals allowed one year, then reversed the tables by setting another record the following season for most powerplay goals scored. Interestingly, both numbers are the same. Name the team and the special-team goals allowed one season and scored the next.

14. Who was the only player during the 1980s to compile 400 penalty minutes in a single season, and how many minutes did he spend in the sin-bin?

15. Who compiled the longest consecutive goal-scoring streak during the 1980s and how many goals did he score during his "red-light" string?

16. Who scored the first overtime goal in regular-season play, when overtime was reinstated in the NHL in 1983?
17. Who was the first NHL defenceman to score 300 career goals?
18. In 1980-81, who became the first player in NHL history to get 30 goals and 300 penalty minutes in the same season?
19. Who was the first player to score 100 points in a season for a team that finished last overall in the NHL?
20. Who was the first player in NHL history to score 60 or more goals in three consecutive seasons?
21. Which NHL veteran played 78 games in 1980-81 without getting a single penalty?
22. Which former veteran was the captain of three NHL teams (Chicago, Los Angeles, and Pittsburgh) in a six-year span?
23. Which player once scored 56 goals in a season without a getting single hat-trick?
24. This former WHL All-Star was the first member of the St. Louis Blues to score 50 goals in a season. Can you name him?
25. This player owns the dubious distinction of playing the most career games in the NHL without scoring a goal. Name him.
26. Who was the last NHL player to lead his team in goals, assists, points, and penalty minutes all in the same season?
27. Who was the last defenceman to lead the NHL in penalty minutes for a season?

28. Which three players tied for the NHL lead in goal scoring during the 1979-80 season?

29. This defenceman became the third NHL blueliner to score 30 goals in a season. Who was the respected rearguard?

30. Who is the only player in NHL history to lead the league in penalty minutes with three different teams during his career?

31. Who holds the NHL record for most penalty minutes in a season by a centre?

32. Name the three members of the Edmonton Oilers who each recorded five-goal games in the 1980s.

33. Who was the first player in NHL history to score a goal in the first, second, third, and overtime periods of the same game?

34. Name the only player to score 50 goals in the minors and 50 goals in the NHL in the 1980s.

35. Who was the second player to score 50 goals in both the NHL and WHA?

36. Who were the four players who recorded 100 points in 50 games or less during the 1980s?

37. Who played the most consecutive games with one team during the 1980s?

38. Who was the last player from the "Original Six" era of the NHL to retire?

39. Who was first NHL coach to win the Jack Adams Award twice?

40. Name the player who took exactly 100 shots during the 1984-85 season and scored exactly one goal.

Answers

1. The Edmonton Oilers went without a loss for the first 15 games of the 1984-85 season, erasing a record established by the Montreal Canadiens in 1942-43.

2. The Montreal Canadiens had 32 straight winning seasons from 1951-52 through 1982-83, and won 16 Stanley Cups during this period. However, the club finished with a poor 35-40-5 record in 1983-84.

3. Paul Reinhart of the Calgary Flames has the distinction of scoring the NHL's 100th penalty-shot goal. Reinhart turned the trick against Ron Low of the New Jersey Devils.

4. The Great One was great at staying in game shape, leading all players by appearing in 774 games in the 1980s, three more than runner-up Mike Gartner.

5. Brad Marsh, who was traded from the Calgary Flames to the Philadelphia Flyers in November 1982, played 83 games in the 1982-83 season, three more than the normal 80-game schedule.

6. Ian Turnbull (four goals vs. Vancouver, December 12, 1981) and Paul Coffey (four goals vs. Calgary on October 26, 1984) are the two rearguards with the quartet of goals.

7. Blair MacDonald spent only six minutes in the penalty box during the 1979-80 season. MacDonald, who spent seven seasons in the WHA, recorded 46 goals and 48 assists for the Edmonton Oilers.

8. Mike Bossy hit the empty cage for his milestone marker on January 2, 1986, while Wayne Gretzky's empty-netter sealed the Oilers' 5-2 victory over Vancouver was the 500th goal of his career.

9. Mario Lemieux won seven games for the Pittsburgh Penguins with an overtime goal in each instance.

10. The St. Louis Blues had ten 20-goal scorers during the 1980-81 season. Brian Sutter (35), Bernie Federko (31), Wayne Babych (54), Jorgen Petterson (37), Blake Dunlop (20), Mike Zuke (24), Perry Turnbull (34), Larry Patey (22), Tony Currie (23), and Blair Chapman (20) all scored at least 20 goals for the Blues during the season.

11. Reed Larson, who played for Detroit, Boston, Edmonton, New York Islanders, Minnesota, and Buffalo during his career, had compiled 685 points when the decade ended.

12. The Winnipeg Jets, who played 99 overtime games since 1983-84 when overtime was reintroduced, won 26 extra-session games in the 1980s.

13. In 1987-88, the Pittsburgh Penguins allowed a record 120 powerplay goals. The following season, they scored 120 powerplay goals of their own to establish another NHL mark.

14. Paul Baxter of the Pittsburgh Penguins collected 409 penalty minutes during the 1981-82 season, the second-highest total in NHL history.

15. Charlie Simmer scored at least one goal in 13 straight games during the 1979-80 season, compiling a total of 17 goals during the string.

16. Bob Bourne scored the overtime winner as the

Islanders beat the Capitals 8-7 in Washington on October 8, 1983. Overtime was last used on November 21, 1942, and was discontinued due to wartime restrictions on train scheduling.

17. Denis Potvin scored career goal 300 during the 1987-88 season with the Islanders. He would eventually total 310 goals in his 15 NHL seasons, all with the Islanders.

18. Vancouver's Tiger Williams had 35 goals to go along with 343 PIM in 1980-81. He was the NHL's first "30-300" player.

19. Joe Sakic finished with 39 goals and 63 assists for 102 points in 1989-90 with Quebec. Quebec finished the season 21st overall with 31 points, last in the league and 33 points behind 20th-place Vancouver.

20. Mike Bossy scored 68 goals in 1980-81, 64 goals in 1981-82, and 60 goals in 1982-83, all with the New York Islanders, the Stanley Cup champions in each of those three seasons.

21. The Islanders' Butch Goring scored 23 goals and 60 points with no penalty minutes for the Islanders in 1980-81.

22. Terry Ruskowski captained, variously, Chicago, Los Angeles, and Pittsburgh between 1981 and 1987.

23. Charlie Simmer of the L.A. Kings scored 56 goals and had 45 assists for 101 points in 1979-80 without recording one three-goal game.

24. Wayne Babych, who scored 54 goals for the Blues

in 1980-81, collected only 75 goals in the rest of his NHL career, which ended in 1986-87.

25. Kim Clackson scored no goals and compiled 370 penalty minutes in 106 games with Pittsburgh and Quebec between 1979 and 1981.

26. Stan Smyl of Vancouver finished the 1979-80 season with 31 goals, 47 assists, 78 points and 204 penalty minutes, the team leader in each of these categories.

27. Randy Holt had 275 penalty minutes, no goals, and eight assists in 70 games as a member of the 1982-83 Washington Capitals.

28. Charlie Simmer (Los Angeles), Danny Gare (Buffalo), and Blaine Stoughton (Hartford) each scored 56 goals in 1979-80.

29. Doug Wilson of Chicago finished with 39 goals and 46 assists for 85 points in 1981-82.

30. Tiger Williams led the NHL in penalty minutes in 1977 (351 minutes) and 1979 (298 minutes) as a Maple Leaf, 1981 (343 minutes) as a Canuck, and in 1987 (358 minutes) as a member of the L.A. Kings.

31. Philadelphia's Ken Linseman set the record for PIM by a centre when he racked up 275 penalty minutes with Philadelphia in 1981-82

32. Wayne Gretzky, Jari Kurri, and Pat Hughes each registered five-goal games for the Edmonton Oilers during the Eighties.

33. Bernie Nicholls scored a goal in each period of the Kings' 5-4 win over Quebec on November 13,

1984, before winning the game with an overtime marker.

34. Joe Mullen scored 59 goals for the Central Hockey League's Salt Lake City Eagles in 1980-81, and later fired 51 goals for the Calgary Flames in their Stanley Cup-winning season in 1988-89.

35. Hartford's Blaine Stoughton became the first member of the Whalers to score 50 goals in an NHL season and second player (Bobby Hull was the other) to score 50 in both the WHA and NHL. Stoughton's 50th came in a 4-4 tie at Vancouver on March 28, 1979.

36. Steve Yzerman, Mario Lemieux, Wayne Gretzky, and Bernie Nicholls all collected 100 points in less than 50 games during the 1980s.

37. Steve Larmer played 560 consecutive games with the Chicago Blackhawks from 1982-83 to 1988-89. Buffalo's Craig Ramsay played 776 straight games with the Sabres, an NHL record for most consecutive games with one team, from the beginning of the 1972-73 season to February 10, 1983, when he broke a bone in his foot.

38. Wayne Cashman, who had played one game for Boston in 1963-64, played eight games in the 1983 playoffs with the Bruins. Serge Savard, who played two games for the Montreal Canadiens in 1966-67, retired after the Winnipeg Jets played three playoffs games in 1982-83. Carol Vadnais, who played 11 games in 1966-67, also retired after the 1982-83 season, but his New Jersey team failed to make the playoffs.

39. In 1988 Jacques Demers became the fifth recipient of the NHL's Jack Adams Award as the league's top coach, when he led the Red Wings to their first division championship since 1965. The next season, 1988-89, the Wings finished atop the Norris Division for the second straight year, and Demers became the first repeat winner of the award.

40. Keith Brown scored just one goal on 100 shots with the Chicago Blackhawks in 1984-85.

Coaching Corner

Match the name of the NHL coach with the team and years he served with that team. Answers on page 134.

Roger Neilson   Chicago, 1987-88

Herb Brooks   Vancouver, 1985-86 to 1986-87

Bob Murdoch   Minnesota, 1987-88

Jacques Martin   Buffalo, 1980-81

Lou Angotti   St. Louis, 1986-87 to 1987-88

Tom Watt   Pittsburgh, 1983-84

5

66 and 99 – The Great Ones

HOCKEY WAS FORTUNATE IN THE 1980s. IT NOT ONLY had one of sport's most dominant athletes in Wayne Gretzky, it had another superstar of equal talent in Mario Lemieux. Gretzky and Lemieux only played together as a unit once in the decade, during the memorable Canada Cup of 1987, but that performance was unequalled in team sport until Earvin "Magic" Johnson and Michael Jordan combined to bring the United States a gold medal in basketball in the 1992 Summer Olympics.

If one name can epitomize the 1980s, that name is Wayne Gretzky. He rewrote the record book "in his image" from the first moment he stepped on the ice. Gretzky's on-ice achievements surpassed any that had occurred before him, and he established himself as the greatest performer in the history of team sport. Indeed, it's easier to mention the records Gretzky didn't break in the 1980s (Sittler's ten-point game, Malone's seven-goal game, and Howe's 801 career goals) than to discuss the marks he did set. However, three records stand above all the rest: his 51-game scoring streak from the start of the season, his 92 goals in one season, and his 163 assists in a single season.

To start a season with 62 goals and 92 assists in 51 games may seem beyond comprehension, yet the record book verifies it as fact. Gretzky accumulated enough points in those 51 games to win the scoring title by 18 points. Although Gretzky's 92-goal season has been approached in the 1990s, all comers have fallen short. When Gretzky established the record, in the 1981-82 season, there was still some debate as to his abilities. The discussion was closed after he opened the next campaign by scoring 50 goals in his first 39 games. The mark remains even more amazing because, by his own admission, Gretzky does not consider himself a scorer.

This is partially true, for there never has been a playmaker of Gretzky's ability. In the 1980s, only one other player, Mario Lemieux, was able to record 100 assists in a season. Gretzky accomplished the feat nine times. In three of those seasons, he accumulated more assists than the next leading scorer had points. The Great One's 163 assists in 1985-86 is 49 more than any other player has been able to compile.

Although Lemieux played only five seasons in the 1980s, he was able to establish himself as Gretzky's equal by the end of the decade. Lemieux hinted at NHL greatness in his first three seasons, but after teaming with Gretzky in the 1987 Canada Cup, Lemieux pushed his game to a new level. In 1987-88, he scored 70 goals and collected 169 points, the highest total by any player other than number 99. In 1988-89, Marvellous Mario came within a single point of the 200-point plateau and joined Wayne Gretzky and Phil Esposito as the only players since Gordie Howe, in 1952-53, to lead the league in goals, assists, and points in one season.

Lemieux's game, while not as polished as Gretzky's, is a combination of crafty intuition and power. Each of his goals is a portrait in pure strength, scored in every imaginable way. No other player can ward off 200-pound defenders and still have the skill to deke the goalie and slip the puck into a vacated cage.

Both Gretzky and Lemieux entered the 1990s at the top of their respective games, and although both have been slowed by injury and illness, they remain the two brightest lights in the NHL sky.

Questions

1. In 1971-72, ten-year-old Wayne Gretzky scored 378 goals as a member of the Nadrofsky Steelers, an Ontario Minor Hockey League (OMHA) "AAA" Novice team. Two of his teammates also went on to play in the NHL. Who were they?
2. In his last season in junior, Mario Lemieux accomplished a feat that has not been equalled since. What is Lemieux's lasting legacy?

3. With which junior team did Wayne Gretzky begin his career, and how many points did he compile in his first stint in the Ontario Hockey League (OHL)?

4. As Mario Lemieux waited in the wings to join the NHL's worst team, Pittsburgh "battled" down to the wire with another team for the right to draft the future superstar. What was the other team and how many points did Pittsburgh finish behind them?

5. Name the former WHA goalie who halted Gretzky's 51-game points streak during the 1983-84 season.

6. In 1988, Mario Lemieux became the fourteenth player to score five goals in a game during the 1980s. However, Lemieux became the first player to score those five goals in five different game situations. How did he score the quintet of markers and who provided the opposition?

7. Who assisted on Gretzky's 1,851st point, a goal that, on October 15, 1989, vaulted him ahead of Gordie Howe as the NHL's all-time leading scorer?

8. In 1989, Mario Lemieux became the second player to score his 50th goal in less than 50 games. How many games did it take for Lemieux to hit the 50-goal plateau and who was the opposing goaltender?

9. When the NHL expanded in 1979-80, the Oilers were allowed to protect four priority selections. One, of course, was the Great One. Who were the other three "original" Oilers?

10. In his final year of junior, Mario Lemieux established a record for consecutive games with at least one point that has never challenged at the junior or professional level. For how many straight games did Lemieux's name appear on the scoresheet, and which QMJHL team finally halted the streak?

11. Wayne Gretzky collected only three major penalties in the 1980s, but the first came in his Lady Byng-winning season in 1979-80. Who was the player with whom the Great One "dropped the gloves?"

12. Shortly after the Rendez-Vous '87 tournament, Mario Lemieux was diagnosed as having bronchitis and was forced to miss a few games. The Penguins dipped into their farm system and promoted the leading scorer on their farm team, the Baltimore Clippers. Who was the player who had to fill Lemieux's skates?

13. When did the first Gretzky vs. Gretzky, brother vs. brother professional hockey confrontation take place? Name the teams involved and where was the game played.

14. Mario Lemieux was the consensus as top pick in the 1984 Entry Draft, but the second player taken also has had an outstanding career. Who was the player who played "second fiddle" to the Lemieux orchestra?

15. Name the three forwards who played on the same line as Wayne Gretzky in 1979-80.

16. Wayne Gretzky scored the most points in the NHL

during the 1980s. Who was the second-highest scorer for the decade?

17. Which NHL player (besides Wayne Gretzky) wore uniform #99 during the 1979-80 season?

18. Which former NHL coach wore uniform #99 in his final NHL season (1980-81)?

19. Whose record did Wayne Gretzky surpass when he collected the 177th post-season point of his career during the 1987 playoffs?

20. In 1988-89, Mario Lemieux broke one of Wayne Gretzky's many records. What was the mark that the Marvellous Mario established?

21. Whose record did Wayne Gretzky break for points in consecutive games?

22. Who was the goalie who surrendered Wayne Gretzky's first NHL goal?

23. Whose team record did Mario Lemieux break to become the Pittsburgh Penguins' all-time leading scorer?

24. How long did it take for Mario Lemieux to score his first NHL goal and who was the goalie who allowed it?

25. On December 15, 1988, Mario Lemieux set a new Penguins record for career assists. Whose mark did he surpass?

26. How many playoff games did Wayne Gretzky play against the New York Islanders before he finally scored a goal against them?

27. Which two junior hockey franchises did Wayne Gretzky own during the 1980s?

28. Which NHL franchise did Wayne Gretzky unflatteringly refer to as a "Mickey Mouse" operation in 1983?

29. In 1988-89, Mario Lemieux won the scoring championship with 199 points and 100 penalty minutes. Name the previous Art Ross Trophy winner who spent 100-or-more minutes in penalty box.

30. From junior through the 1980s, Wayne Gretzky was the top scorer on his team on every occasion but one. Can you name the team Gretzky played for that exceptional season and the player who surpassed his scoring totals?

31. Wayne Gretzky's first pro hockey coach had a son who played 99 games in the 1980s. Who was the coach and who was his hockey-playing son?

32. Mario Lemieux's last junior coach later followed him to the NHL. Who was the Marvellous One's last junior bench boss?

33. Despite playing for one of the top junior teams in Canada, only one of Mario Lemieux's teammates on the Laval Voisins followed him to the NHL. Who was the player and which team selected him in the NHL Draft?

34. How many goals did Mario Lemieux score in the 1987 Canada Cup tournament and how many of his goals were set up by Wayne Gretzky?

Answers

1. Goaltender Greg Stefan and linemate Len Hachborn both played in the NHL. Stefan spent nine seasons with Detroit, while Hachborn, after stints with the Flyers and the Kings, is still active with the San Diego Gulls of the IHL, where he is one of the team's leading scorers.
2. In 1983-84, Lemieux led the QMJHL in goals, assists, and points in both the regular season and the playoffs.
3. Gretzky began his major junior career with the OHL's Peterborough Petes, playing a three-game trial as an injury replacement during the 1976-77 season. Gretzky collected three assists in the three games before returning to the Toronto Nats.
4. The New Jersey Devils finished with 41 points, three more than the Penguins, despite losing their last eight games. The Penguins lost 17 of their last 20 games.
5. Markus Mattson of the Los Angeles Kings stopped Gretzky's streak with a 4-2 victory over the Oilers, January 28, 1984.
6. Lemieux scored a goal on a breakaway, power-play, penalty shot, shorthanded, and into an empty net on New Year's Eve, 1988, against the New Jersey Devils' Chris Terreri and Bob Sauve.
7. Steve Duchesne and Dave Taylor set up the decisive goal, which was scored in dramatic fashion against his former Edmonton Oiler teammates in the last minute of play.

8. Lemieux scored his 50th goal in the Penguins' 46th game (it was Lemieux's 44th game) against the Winnipeg Jets and Eldon "Pokey" Reddick. The date was January 20, 1989. Pittsburgh won 7-3.

9. The Oilers protected goaltenders Dave Dryden and Eddie Mio, and centre Bengt Gustaffson.

10. Lemieux registered a point in 61 straight games before the Verdun Juniors of the QMJHL shut him off the board in a 3-1 victory over Lemieux's Laval teammates.

11. In a 6-4 victory over the Chicago Blackhawks on March 14, 1980, Gretzky and Hawks winger Doug Lecuyer went "toe-to-toe" in the second period.

12. The Penguins promoted Mario's brother, Alain, who was having his finest professional season in 1986-87. However, he played only one game for the Penguins during his brother's absence, ironically the last NHL game he would play.

13. Wayne and Keith Gretzky faced off against each other in the opening draw of a Buffalo-Edmonton exhibition game held in Halifax, Nova Scotia, on September 24, 1985. Edmonton won the match 2-1 with the winning goal supplied by Wayne. Keith, a Buffalo Sabre draft selection in 1985, was held off the scoresheet.

14. Kirk Muller, the all-time leading scorer of the New Jersey Devils and currently a member of the defending Stanley Cup champion Montreal Canadiens, was the Devils' top choice in the 1984 lottery.

15. Brett Callighen (58 points) and Blair MacDonald (94 points) were Gretzky's linemates. However, in the final weeks of the season, Callighen was injured and the Oilers traded Bobby Schmautz to the Colorado Rockies for Don Ashby, who collected 19 points in 18 games playing on a line with Gretzky.

16. Peter Stastny of Quebec finished the 1980s with 986 points, as the decade's second-leading scorer. Gretzky led the way with 1,837 points.

17. Wilf Paiement wore 99 for a time with Toronto in 1979-80.

18. Rick Dudley wore 99 with Winnipeg in 1980-81.

19. Jean Beliveau of the Canadiens scored 176 playoff points during his 20-year NHL career.

20. Mario Lemieux set an NHL record with 13 shorthanded goals in 1988-89, breaking the record of 12 set by Wayne Gretzky with Edmonton in 1983-84.

21. Guy Lafleur scored in 28 consecutive games in 1976-77. Gretzky first broke the record with 30 straight games with a point in 1982-83 before establishing the current mark of 51 consecutive games in 1983-84.

22. Glen Hanlon of the Vancouver Canucks was the victim of Gretzky's first NHL goal on October 14, 1979, when the Oilers tied Vancouver 4-4 at Edmonton.

23. On December 6, 1989, Mario Lemieux scored his 317th NHL goal to surpass Jean Pronovost, as the Penguins' all-time goal-scoring leader. It came in

his 395th game, and paced the Penguins to a 5-3 win over Washington at the Civic Arena.

24. Mario Lemieux scored one minute into his first shift in his first NHL game, stealing the puck from Boston's Ray Bourque and scoring an unassisted goal on Pete Peeters at the 2:59 mark of the first period, October 11, 1984.

25. Lemieux's 350th career assist broke Syl Apps, Jr.'s team mark established between 1971 and 1979.

26. Gretzky was held without a goal in his first eleven playoff games against the Islanders, dating back to their first series in 1981. He finally "solved" Billy Smith in game four of the 1984 Stanley Cup finals.

27. The Great One purchased 45% of the OHL's Belleville Bulls in 1982 and sold his shares in 1984. In 1985, he purchased the Hull Olympiques of the QMJHL and became the team's president.

28. Gretzky, who rarely puts his skate in his mouth, was referring to the New Jersey Devils, who the Oilers had just defeated 13-4. Gretzky had eight points against his good friend, Devils' goalie Ron Low, and was upset at the lack of support for his former teammate by the Devils' backcheckers.

29. Lemieux became the first player since Bobby Orr to win the scoring title despite having spent 100 minutes in the penalty box. Lemieux had exactly 100 PIM in 1988-89, while Orr collected 101 PIM in 1974-75.

30. During the 1978-79 WHA season, Wayne Gretzky had a brief eight-game stay with the Indianapolis

Racers, accumulating six points. The team disbanded after 25 games. Blaine Stoughton was the team's leading scorer with nine goals and nine assists. Gretzky finished the season with Edmonton, totalling 110 points. Stoughton played the rest of the 1978-79 campaign with New England, scoring a total of 30 points.

31. When Gretzky turned professional with the WHA's Indianapolis Racers, his coach was former Blackhawks' defenceman Pat Stapleton. His son, Mike, also played for the Blackhawks in the 1980s.

32. Pierre Creamer, Mario Lemieux's coach at Laval, was the Pittsburgh Penguins coach during the 1987-88 season.

33. Defenceman Steven Finn was picked 57th pick overall in the third round of the 1984 Entry Draft by the Quebec Nordiques.

34. Mario scored 11 goals during the 1987 Canada Cup, nine of which were set up by Gretzky. Michel Goulet and Craig Hartsburg set up the rest.

Word Puzzle

Find words in letter puzzle below. Words can be found horizontally, vertically, diagonally, spelled frontward or backward. Solution on page 136.

```
C J X U E I M E L O I R A M C
H O C K E Y Z R S A P T M O W
L H L P B F R E E A G E N T A
Y N A O E T B C M T N Q X D Y
E Z R W R F J H A I T S L H N
Y I E L N A P O L P U U V C E
S E H E I R D G F A T S S Z G
S G T J E D I O Y H G A D F R
O L A P F Y C A R E D L I N E
B E S E E R I L A O K L Z N T
E R N N D T N L G P C X C V Z
K R E A E N G I L A M K N B K
I T L L R E Y N A S U I I O Y
M H G T K G F E C S D S A E P
J K O Y O R K C I R T A P W S
```

Bernie Federko
Calgary Flames
Captain
Colorado Rockies
Entry Draft
Free Agent
Glen Sather

Goalline
Hockey
Icing
John Ziegler
Mario Lemieux
Mike Bossy

NHL
Pass
Patrick Roy
Penalty
Redline
Sutter
Wayne Gretzky

6

A Decade of All-Stars

IN THE 1980s, SOME OF THE FINEST TALENT TO EVER play the game of hockey starred in the NHL. When the league expanded in 1979-80 to include four former WHA franchises, it gave the opportunity for some of that league's best players to showcase their skills in the NHL. Players such as Wayne Gretzky, Mike Liut, Mark Messier, Mark Howe, and John Tonelli all arrived in the NHL after beginning their pro careers in the WHA and all went on to become first- or second-team NHL All-Stars.

The NHL's All-Star squads in the 1980s were dominated by two players: Wayne Gretzky and Ray Bourque, each of whom appeared on either the league's first or second All-Star teams in every year of the decade. Gretzky earned seven first-team berths while Bourque was selected as a first-team All-Star on six occasions. The dominant right-winger of the decade was Mike Bossy, who earned six All-Star team selections before a back injury forced him to retire after only ten NHL seasons. Jari Kurri was a five-time member of the all-star assembly, while other notables such as Dave Taylor, Rick Middleton, Tim Kerr, and Joe Mullen earned single All-Star berths.

In 1982-83, the first All-Rookie team was selected with future NHL stars like Phil Housley, Scott Stevens, and Steve Larmer meriting inclusion on the six-member squad. Since that time, the freshman All-Star squad has included such outstanding young talent such as Patrick Roy, Tom Barrasso, Mario Lemieux, Luc Robitaille, and Brian Leetch, each of whom has also earned spots on the NHL's first All-Star team.

The NHL's annual mid-season showdown, the All-Star Game, continued to be hockey's finest one-day assemblage of talent. During the decade, the Wales Conference won six of the ten All-Star contests, with Mario Lemieux and Wayne Gretzky each winning a pair of All-Star MVP awards. The Great One set an All-Star record in 1983 with four goals in the third period while Lemieux earned one his "stars" with a six-point effort, including the overtime winner, in 1988.

The concept of the mid-season classic changed in 1989 when the NHL introduced its All-Star Weekend. Combining a skills competition focused on shooting, skating, and scoring, as well as a Heroes of Hockey game and the All-Star Game itself, the weekend package was met with great enthusiasm. The league attained a high profile for this event after the NBC network signed a deal to broadcast the All-Star Game throughout the United States.

Late in the 1988-89 season, the NHL and the Soviet Hockey Federation reached an agreement that enabled the finest Soviet players to join the NHL, making the NHL the first truly global sports league. With Russian stars like Makarov, Fetisov, Mogilny, Bure, Kamensky, and Fedorov entering the NHL in the 1990s, another decade of all-star performances is assured.

Questions

1. How many different goaltenders earned a berth on the NHL's First All-Star Team during the 1980s and how many of the active netminders are still with the same club?
2. Who was the only centreman other than Gretzky and Lemieux to earn a berth on the NHL's First All-Star Team in the 1980s?
3. Who holds the All-Star Game mark for most assists in a single game during the 1980s?
4. This member of the NHL's All-Rookie Team was the 129th player selected in the 1983 Entry Draft but played only 59 NHL games since earning the rookie honour. Who was he?
5. Who was the first player in Calgary Flames' franchise history to earn a selection to the First All-Star Team?
6. How many goals did Wayne Gretzky score in All-Star competition during the 1980s?

7. Who is the only member of the NHL's All-Rookie Team to be traded midway through his rookie campaign?

8. Who was the only member of the St. Louis Blues to earn a place on the league's First All-Star Team in the 1980s?

9. In the four seasons between 1983-84 and 1986-87, Michel Goulet earned three First Team All-Star nominations. However, in 1984-85, he was bumped by a left-winger who earned, as it turned out, the only All-Star berth of his career. Who was the lucky left-winger?

10. Four different defencemen earned at least two First Team All-Star nominations during the 1980s. Name them.

11. Before Wayne Gretzky exploded for four goals in the third period of the 1983 All-Star Game, officials had already selected another player as the game's MVP. Who was the player who took a backseat to Gretzky in the MVP spotlight, and who was the goalie who surrendered Wayne's four goals?

12. When Wayne Gretzky won yet another automotive vehicle as the All-Star Game MVP in 1989, he surprised many fans by announcing he was giving his prize away. Who did he give the truck to and why?

13. Only three rookies were named to the NHL's First All-Star Team in the 1980s. Name them and the years in which they earned their honours.

14. This "oldster" made the NHL's All-Rookie Team a

full ten years after he was selected in the league's amateur draft. Who was the late-blooming freshman and who originally selected him in the draft?

15. This two-time All-Star Game participant was born in Timmins, Ontario, but played his first pro hockey in Sweden after graduating from Notre Dame, where he was a Central Collegiate Hockey Association (CCHA) All-Star. Who is this European-flavoured All-Star?

16. This All-Star rearguard was the only defenceman since 1969 to have won the Norris Trophy with fewer than 73 scoring points. Who was he?

17. Name this four-time participant in the All-Star Game who was the first player to score over 200 goals for two different NHL teams.

18. This perennial All-Star was one of only two NHL players to score at least 40 goals and register at least 50 assists in seven straight seasons, from 1982-83 to 1988-89. Wayne Gretzky was one, who was the other?

19. After an eight-year retirement from the NHL, this All-Star came back at age 41 during the 1979-80 season to play for Toronto. Who was he?

20. This Hall of Famer played in the NHL All-Star Game in both 1969 and 1984. Can you recall his name?

21. Name his All-Star rearguard who got off to the fastest start ever by an NHL defenceman, scoring 10 goals in his first 15 games in 1987-88.

22. Who was the first player – goaltenders excluded

– to win the Calder Trophy and be named to the First Team All-Stars in the same season?

23. These two All-Stars, who were drafted in the same year and scored 1,245 goals between them, lined up together as regular-season teammates for the first time on October 24, 1988. Who were they?

24. This former All-Star defenceman came out of retirement on February 12, 1981, with Colorado and immediately became the oldest player in the NHL. Who was he?

25. On October 5, 1981, the Winnipeg Jets acquired this veteran defenceman from the Montreal Canadiens. They traded him back to Montreal two seasons later. Who was the All-Star rearguard and who did the Jets receive when they sent him back to the Habs?

26. This All-Star defenceman was the first rearguard in NHL history to score two shorthanded goals in one regular-season period. Can you name him?

27. This All-Star defenceman established the longest consecutive point-scoring streak by a blueliner in 1986. Who was the reliable rearguard and in how many games did he collect at least one point?

28. Which four-time member of the NHL's First All-Star Team went three years, 11 months, and 22 days between goals?

29. At the 1989 All-Star Game in Edmonton, the Oilers appointed two honourary captains who had never played for Edmonton's NHL team. Who were they?

30. Who is the youngest goaltender to appear in an All-Star Game?
31. Who was the MVP of the 1984 All-Star Game and how many points did he record in the game?
32. Who is the only rookie to win All-Star Game MVP honours?
33. Two All-Star Games during the 1980s went into overtime. Who scored the winning goals in these two mid-season classics?
34. Fan balloting for the All-Star Game began in 1986. Who gathered the most votes in the first year of voting?
35. In the 1980 All-Star Game, eleven future members of the Hockey Hall of Fame were among the 40 players taking part in the contest. How many of their names can you remember?

Answers

1. Ten different goalies (Esposito, Smith, Liut, Peeters, Barrasso, Lindbergh, Vanbiesbrouck, Hextall, Fuhr, and Roy) were selected as First Team All-Stars. Only Patrick Roy of the Montreal Canadiens is still with the same team.
2. Marcel Dionne, who won his only Art Ross Trophy in 1979-80, was the league's All-Star centre in Gretzky's first NHL season.
3. Mats Naslund recorded five assists for the Wales Conference in the Wales's 6-5 win over their

Campbell counterparts in the 1988 All-Star Game.

4. The Winnipeg Jets' Iain Duncan, whose sophomore season was actually better than his rookie campaign, has played only two NHL games since 1988-89.

5. Hakan Loob, who scored 50 goals in 1987-88, was selected as the NHL's best right-winger after a 106-point season for the Flames.

6. The Great One scored 10 goals in nine All-Star Games, including a 1980s record of four in the 1983 All-Star tilt.

7. Dan Daoust, a member of the first NHL All-Rookie squad in 1983, was dealt to the Toronto Maple Leafs by the Montreal Canadiens in December 1982.

8. Mike Liut, who finished as the runner-up to Wayne Gretzky in the Hart Trophy race in 1980-81, was the First Team All-Star for the Blues.

9. John Ogrodnick, who had never earned an All-Star berth in junior or professional hockey, won the left-winger's spot on the NHL's First All-Star Team in 1984-85 after scoring 55 goals and 105 points for Detroit.

10. Ray Bourque (6), Paul Coffey (3), Mark Howe (2), and Rod Langway (2) were the NHL's most honoured rearguards during the 1980s.

11. John Garrett was the original winner of the 1983 All-Star Game MVP award, before Gretzky fired four goals in the final 20 minutes to steal the

spotlight. Pelle Lindbergh allowed seven goals, including Gretzky's four, during the game.

12. After winning the All-Star Game MVP award in the 1989 game in Edmonton in front of his former fans and teammates, Gretz gave his MVP truck to former teammate Dave Semenko as thanks for Semenko's role in making him the NHL's all-time leading scorer. The newly retired Semenko had been Gretzky's on-ice protector during Gretzky's stint with the Oilers.

13. Ray Bourque was named to the NHL's First All-Star Team in 1979-80, Tom Barrasso earned a berth on the squad in 1983-84, and Ron Hextall won the same honour in 1986-87.

14. Warren Young, originally drafted by California in 1975, played for Minnesota before catching on with Pittsburgh, where he scored 40 goals in 1985.

15. Dave Poulin, signed as a free agent by Philadelphia in March 1983, played in the 1986 and 1988 All-Star Games after returning from Sweden, where he had 62 points in 32 games.

16. Rod Langway of the Washington Capitals won the Norris Trophy with 32 points in 1983, and 33 points in 1984.

17. Lanny McDonald scored 219 goals with Toronto between 1973 and 1979 and 215 goals with the Flames between 1981 and 1989.

18. Jari Kurri of the Oilers scored at least 40 goals and 50 assists each season between 1982-83 and 1988-89.

19. Carl Brewer, a First Team All-Star with Toronto in 1962-63, came out of retirement in 1979-80, and played 20 games for the Leafs at the age of 41.
20. Brad Park represented the New York Rangers in the 1969 All-Star Game and represented the Detroit Red Wings in the 1984 mid-season classic.
21. Phil Housley of the Sabres scored 10 goals in his first 15 games in 1987-88 and finished the season with 29 goals and 37 assists for 66 points in 74 games.
22. Boston defenceman Ray Bourque capped a great rookie season in 1979-80 by being named both the winner of the Calder Trophy and a member of the First All-Star Team. He was the first non-goalie to win both honours in his rookie year.
23. Guy Lafleur and Marcel Dionne, 1971 draftees, each scored a goal as linemates for the first time in the Rangers' 4-1 win over Washington. It was Dionne's first goal of the year, and the second for Lafleur.
24. Terry Harper, the Colorado Rockies' 41-year-old assistant coach, came out of retirement to help the Rockies tie Pittsburgh 3-3.
25. The Jets obtained Serge Savard from Montreal in the 1981 NHL Waiver Draft and later traded him back to Montreal for Peter Taglianetti. Savard became the Canadiens' managing director upon his return from the Jets.
26. Mark Howe fired the two shorthanded markers during an 8-6 loss to the St. Louis Blues October 9, 1980.
27. On January 25, 1986, Paul Coffey recorded a point

in his 28th consecutive game and established the NHL's longest point streak by a defenceman. The streak, which dated back to November 17, 1985, saw Coffey register 16 goals and 39 assists in the 28-game span.

28. After three years of retirement, Guy Lafleur scored his first goal as a New York Ranger and added an assist in the Rangers 3-2 win over the Vancouver Canucks on October 16, 1988.

29. Bruce MacGregor, who spent two seasons with the WHA Oilers, and Norm Ullman, who also spent two campaigns with the WHA team, were the honourary captains.

30. Grant Fuhr was 19 years old when he played the first 30 minutes of the 1982 All-Star Game at the Cap Center in Washington.

31. Don Maloney, who had never had a four-point night in his career, scored one goal and added three assists to win MVP honours at the 36th annual All-Star Game.

32. Mario Lemieux, with two goals and one assist in the Wales Conference's 6-4 win over the Campbells, won MVP honours in 1985.

33. Bryan Trottier scored the overtime winner at 3:05 in 1986 and Mario Lemieux fired the extra-session decider at 1:08 in 1987.

34. Paul Coffey collected 309,503 votes in 1986 to lead all vote getters.

35. The eleven "Famers" were Marcel Dionne, Bob Gainey, Gordie Howe, Gil Perreault, Jean Ratelle, Darryl Sittler, Bill Barber, Mike Bossy, Phil Esposito, and Tony Esposito.

The Ron Francis Show

Number the following photos of Ron Francis in chronological order, youngest to oldest. Answers on page 134.

A

B

C

D

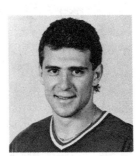
E

Beyond the Borders

THE NHL OPENED ITS DOORS TO THE WORLD IN the 1980s, and the world responded by sending its best hockey players to North America to join the world's greatest hockey league. The NHL's international invasion actually began close to home, when scouts and general managers began to pay greater attention to American-born players, both from the college and high-school systems. In the midst of the NHL-WHA bidding war in the late 1970s, NHL officials turned to the U.S. for talent, drafting a record 73 players from American colleges in 1978. However, the majority of those selections came in the later rounds and only a handful – Craig MacTavish, Dave Silk, Chris Nilan, and Tom Laidlaw – had noteworthy careers in the NHL.

Although only 15 players were drafted from American colleges the following season, it took the success of the U.S. Olympic Team in the 1980 Winter Games to firmly establish the U.S. as a rich resource of hockey talent. The 1980 team sent a number of top-notch players like Neal Broten, Dave Christian, Ken Morrow, Craig Ramsay, and Mark Johnson into the NHL immediately after the conclusion of the Lake Placid Games. That success encouraged NHL teams to choose two American players first overall in the draft, with Brian Lawton being selected number one in 1983 Entry Draft and Mike Modano earning the first overall selection in 1988. By the end of the decade, American-born players such as Pat LaFontaine, Ed Olczyk, Chris Chelios, Tom Barrasso, and Brian Leetch were recognized as being among the finest in the league.

The European invasion, which was a key feature of the WHA in the 1970s, was accelerated by the NHL in the 1980s. Only six European players were drafted in 1979. By the end of the decade, that number had grown to 38, imports having arrived yearly from Sweden, Finland, and Czechoslovakia. The international road opened by Borje Salming, Anders Hedberg, and Vaclav Nedomansky in the 1970s paved the way for future NHL stars like Jari Kurri, Peter Stastny, Pelle Lindbergh, Hakan Loob, Kent Nilsson, and Tomas Sandstrom in the 1980s. By the end of the decade, Russian-trained players began arriving in the NHL, providing the league with a wider talent pool than ever before.

The international highlights of the decade were the three Canada Cup competitions, held in 1981,

1984, and 1987. In 1981, the Soviet Union showed why they were the world's top hockey power by easily dispatching Canada 8-1 in the championship final. The one-sided score was disappointing, and a far cry from the end-to-end action that was a common feature of the Russia-Canada international showcases in the 1970s. However, the latter two tournaments produced the most exciting hockey of the decade, with Canada and the Soviet Union engaging in four memorable games that illustrated why hockey is the most exciting of team sports. In 1984, a superb effort by Paul Coffey to break up a Soviet two-on-one rush in overtime of the semi-final paved the way for Mike Bossy's overtime winner. In 1987, all three games in the tournament final were decided by identical 6-5 scores, with two of the contests needing overtime to decide. Mario Lemieux's dramatic goal and broadcaster Dan Kelly's energized description of it in the pivotal third contest, remain two of the game's most treasured moments of the decade.

Questions

1. During the 1980s, the Central Red Army team lost only five games to NHL competition. One team beat them twice, once in 1980 and again in 1989. Which team "solved" the Soviets?
2. During the 1980s, four different Soviet teams played against NHL competition. Name the four teams?

3. Who was the first NHL goalie to defeat the powerful Central Red Army team in an exhibition series in the 1980s?

4. Who were the only two Canadian players to earn berths on the Canada Cup All-Star Team after the 1981 Canada Cup tournament?

5. Who was the MVP of the 1984 Canada Cup tournament?

6. In the 1988 Winter Olympics, professional athletes were allowed to compete for the first time. Six NHL players suited up to play in the Olympic Games for Canada. Who were they?

7. Six members of the U.S. Olympic Team that captured the gold medal in 1980 were still playing in the NHL when the decade was over. Name them.

8. In the opener of the two game Rendez-Vous '87 tournament, Team NHL scored in the final minute to squeeze out a 4-3 win. Who fired the winning marker for the All-Stars?

9. The first Soviet-trained goaltender to play in the NHL made his international debut against NHL competition in 1985. Who was he?

10. Who is the NHL's leading scorer among players who competed in the Olympics in the 1980s?

11. Name five members of the 1984 Canadian Olympic Team still active in the NHL at the end of the 1980s who went directly to the NHL from the Olympics without playing in the minors.

12. Which two future NHL All-Stars and award winners graduated directly to the NHL from the U.S. Olympic Team in 1984?

13. Of the six European goaltenders who appeared in the 1987 Canada Cup tournament, who was the first to play in the NHL?

14. Name the three European-trained goaltenders who were on the NHL roster when the 1979-80 season opened.

15. Who was the only goaltender to defeat the Soviets twice in super-series competition during the 1980s ?

16. Name the NHL All-Star born in Taiwan.

17. Who was the only player to suit up for the NHL in 1987-88 who had his hockey training in West Germany?

18. Who was the first Swedish player to score 50 goals in an NHL season?

19. Who was the first U.S.-born player to jump to the NHL directly out of high school hockey?

20. Who was the first U.S.-born player to score 100 points in an NHL season?

21. Who was the first European-trained player to score 100 points in an NHL season?

22. Who was the first U.S.-born player to score 50 goals in an NHL season?

23. This veteran, born in Grostenquin, France, scored at least 30 goals in eight of his ten NHL seasons for three different teams. Who was the well-travelled marksman?

24. Who were the first American-born coaches to oppose each other in an NHL game?

25. This 14-year NHL veteran, born in Garnant, South

Wales, became the coach the Hartford Whalers on June 7, 1983. Name him.

26. Who was the first Soviet-trained player to score a goal in the NHL?

27. Who was the first American-born player to score 200 goals in the NHL?

28. Who was the first American-born player to record 50 goals and 50 assists in the same season?

29. Which American-born player scored 269 goals in the 1980s using his own brand of hockey stick?

30. Which future NHL goalie registered a 3-4 mark as the starting goalie for Dynamo Riga during the 1988-89 Super Series?

31. Name the first European drafted in round one of the NHL entry draft during the 1980s?

32. Name the only player to be selected in the NHL entry draft from the British Ice Hockey League.

33. During the 1980s, American-born players have won First Team All-Star berths six times. One player leads the way with three selections, while three other players have been chosen once. Can you name these players ?

34. During the 1980s, eight European-trained rookies have been named to the NHL's All-Rookie Team. How many of their names can you recall?

35. Which current NHL coach played in Japan before returning to North America to become a 40-goal scorer in his rookie NHL season?

Answers

1. The Buffalo Sabres defeated Red Army 6-1 on January 3, 1980, and 6-5 on January 9, 1989.
2. Central Red Army, Dynamo Moscow, Dynamo Riga, and the Soviet All-Star Selects played NHL teams.
3. Richard Sevigny allowed only two goals as the Montreal Canadiens downed the Red Army 4-2 on New Year's Eve, 1979. Vladislav Tretiak earned a lengthy standing ovation from the Montreal fans before and after the game.
4. Mike Bossy and Gil Perreault were each named to the tournament All-Star squad. Despite leading the series in scoring, Wayne Gretzky was left off the team, replaced by Sergei Shepelev.
5. John Tonelli, who recorded three goals and six assists in eight games, was named as the MVP of the Canada Cup '84 showdown.
6. Serge Boisvert (Montreal), Jim Peplinski (Calgary), Randy Gregg (Edmonton), Brian Bradley (Vancouver), Steve Tambellini (Vancouver), and Andy Moog (Boston) were all NHL professionals who were given permission to play for Canada at the 1988 Winter Olympic Games in Calgary.
7. Neal Broten (Minnesota), Dave Christian (Winnipeg, Washington), Mark Johnson (Pittsburgh, Minnesota, Hartford, St. Louis, New Jersey), Ken Morrow (New York Islanders), Jack O'Callahan (Chicago, New Jersey), and Mike Ramsey

(Buffalo) were the U.S. Olympians still active when the 1980s came to a close.

8. Dave Poulin redirected a nice feed from Mario Lemieux past goaltender Evgeny Belosheiken with 1:15 remaining in the third period to give Canada a 4-3 victory in the lid-lifter of the Rendez-Vous '87 series.

9. Sergei Mylnikov, who replaced Vladislav Tretiak as the number-one goalie for the Central Red Army team in 1985, played 10 games for the Quebec Nordiques in 1989-90.

10. Glenn Anderson, who collected his 1,000th NHL point in March, 1993, played for the 1980 Canadian Olympic Team and finished second in scoring to Kevin Maxwell.

11. Russ Courtnall, Doug Lidster, Dave Tippett, James Patrick, and Bob Brooke remained in the NHL without any minor-league tutoring.

12. Both Pat LaFontaine and Chris Chelios went directly to the NHL without any minor-league playing time. Both Al Iafrate and Ed Olczyk reached the NHL as well, but not until the following season.

13. Kari Takko, who appeared in five games for Team Finland in the '87 Canada Cup series, played 39 games for the Minnesota North Stars in 1985-86 and 1986-87.

14. Hardy Astrom (Colorado), Jiri Crha (Toronto), Goran Hogosta (Quebec).

15. Don Edwards was in goal when the Buffalo Sabres defeated Red Army 4-2 during the 1979-80

season and was with Calgary when the Flames downed the Soviet All-Stars 3-2 in 1983.

16. Rod Langway, who played 15 seasons with Washington and Montreal, was born in Formosa, Taiwan, on May 3, 1957.

17. Uwe Krupp was born in Cologne, West Germany and played for Kölner Eishockey Club in Cologne before joining Buffalo in the NHL.

18. Hakan Loob, who was born in Visby, Sweden, finished with 50 goals and 56 assists for 106 points during the 1987-88 season for Calgary.

19. Bobby Carpenter joined the Washington Capitals in 1981-82, after scoring 38 points in 18 games for St. John's High School in Massachusetts the year before.

20. Neal Broten, born in Roseau, Minnesota, got an assist in a 6-1 win over Toronto on March 26, 1986, to become the first U.S.-born player to score 100 points in a season. He finished the season with 29 goals and 76 assists for 105 points for Minnesota.

21. Kent Nilsson, who was born in Nynashamn, Sweden, scored 49 goals and 82 assists for 131 points with Calgary in 1980-81. His 100th point came on the second goal of a hat-trick in a 5-1 win over Hartford on February 27, 1981.

22. Bobby Carpenter, who was born in Beverly, Massachusetts, scored 53 goals and 42 assists for 95 points for Washington in the 1984-85 season, to become the first U.S.-born player to get 50

goals. Goal number 50 came in a 3-2 loss to Montreal on March 21, 1985.

23. Paul MacLean scored 30 or more goals eight times in nine seasons with St. Louis, Winnipeg, and Detroit, before retiring 37 games into his tenth season.

24. On February 22, 1981, Larry Pleau's Hartford Whalers defeated Craig Patrick's New York Rangers by a 6-5 score in the NHL's first all-American coaching match-up.

25. Jack Evans, who played with Chicago and the New York Rangers and later coached in California and Cleveland, was the fifth head coach of the Hartford Whalers.

26. Victor Nachaev helped the Kings to a 5-3 win at New York on October 17, 1982. On October 16, 1982, Nachaev became the first Soviet-trained player to play in an NHL game, although he went scoreless for the L.A. Kings in a 4-1 loss to the Islanders at New York. He had defected to the U.S. with his American-born wife and played a total of three games in the NHL.

27. Reed Larson became the first American-born player and the sixth defenceman in NHL history to score 200 career goals in a 6-4 win against the Whalers on January 15, 1987.

28. Jimmy Carson became the first U.S.-born player to score 50 goals and 50 assists in a season when he recorded his 55th goal and 51st assist on March 30, 1988.

29. Dave Christian's father and uncle (Bill and Roger, respectively) own The Christian Bros. Stick Co. in Warroad, Minnesota. Bill and Roger were members of the gold medal-winning U.S. Olympic Team in 1960. Dave was a member of the "Miracle on Ice" team in 1980.

30. Arturs Irbe, originally selected by Minnesota in the 1989 Entry Draft, was the San Jose Sharks' top goalie in 1992-93.

31. Jiri Dudacek of the Kladno team in Czechoslovakia was selected 17th overall by the Buffalo Sabres in the 1981 draft.

32. In the 1986 Entry Draft, the Edmonton Oilers selected British-trained hockey star Tony Hand 252nd overall from the roster of the Murrayfield Racers.

33. Mark Howe of the Philadelphia Flyers was chosen three times, in 1982-83, 1985-86, and 1986-87. Single First Team selections were awarded to Tom Barrasso (1983-84), Chris Chelios (1988-89), and Joe Mullen (1988-89).

34. The "big eight" are Pelle Lindbergh (1983), Mats Naslund (1983), Hakan Loob (1984), Thomas Eriksson (1984), Tomas Sandstrom (1985), Kjell Dahlin (1986), Calle Johansson (1988), and David Volek (1989).

35. Darryl Sutter played a season in Japan before returning to Canada late in the 1978-79 campaign to join the AHL's New Brunswick Hawks. Currently the coach of the Chicago Blackhawks, Sutter scored 40 goals in his first NHL season in 1980-81.

Careering Along

The following players born outside North America played for a variety of clubs in the NHL during the 1980s. Match each player with the correct team or teams. (In the case of players who dressed for more than one club, team names are listed in chronological order.) Answers on page 135.

Helmut Balderis   Minnesota

Raimo Summanen   St. Louis, Hartford, Washington

Jiri Bubla   NY Islanders, Minnesota

Mats Hallin   Edmonton, Vancouver

Jorgen Pettersson   Vancouver

Anders Eldebrink   Vancouver, Quebec

The Last Line of Defence

THE 1980s WERE YEARS OF CHANGE FOR NHL GOAL-tenders. The three-goaltender system was introduced in the early part of the decade. Although teams in the 1970s often used more than two goaltenders in a single season, the teams of the 1980s often utilized three goaltenders on a regular rotating basis. In 1980-81, for the first time in league history, the Vezina Trophy was shared by three goaltenders, with Montreal's Richard Sevigny, Denis Herron, and Michel Larocque carving their names on the award. However, near the end of the decade, iron-men such as Ron Hextall and Grant Fuhr and tandems like Moog-Lemelin, Vanbiesbrouck-Froese, and Vernon-Wamsley allowed teams to play with two goalies.

Goaltenders also took a more active role in creating offense during the decade. Added emphasis was placed on netminders to develop stickhandling and shooting skills, which allowed the goalie to clear the zone accurately and pass the puck to fast-breaking forwards. Grant Fuhr set an NHL record with 14 assists in 1983-84, out-scoring dozens of regulars alone the way. Ron Hextall, perhaps the goaltending fraternity's most accurate marksman, shot and scored twice during the decade, a feat which has yet to be equalled.

Perhaps the greatest changes in the art of goaltending revolve around the modernization of equipment. Alterations in face masks, blockers and trappers, pads, and body armour gave the goalie added flexibility and protection, while greatly reducing the weight the goalie had to carry throughout the game. By the mid-1980s, nearly every goaltender wore a cage attached to a decorated fiberglass mask. The cage mask allowed goaltenders a greater range of peripheral vision, especially useful in locating pucks at their feet. Another recent innovation is the throat protector which hangs from the chin of the face mask. Yet another innovation has been the introduction of foam-filled goalie pads. This new lightweight leg protection allows goalies to drop to their knees and bounce back up on their skates quicker. The pads also repell moisture and don't become water-logged like the old pads stuffed with deerhair.

Although the regular season throughout the 1980s were dominated by offense, when the playoffs rolled around, goaltenders were once again the key to Stanley Cup success. The Islanders Billy Smith was at his best in the playoffs, establishing records for playoff games and minutes played. Grant Fuhr, too, came to be regarded as one of hockey's best big-game goaltenders. Fuhr, who was often left to fend for himself while his teammates performed their offensive wizardry at the other end of the ice, refused to give up that extra goal, a trait that has earned him five Stanley Cup rings. Patrick Roy, who won the Conn Smythe Trophy at age 20 in 1986, established himself as the league's top goaltender as the decade came to a close.

Already the 1990s has produced a number of noteworthy young goaltenders including Ed Belfour, Felix Potvin, and Tommy Soderstrom, insuring that the NHL's last line of defence will remain its first line of excellence.

Questions

1. Four goaltenders played for four NHL teams from 1979-80 to 1988-89. Can you name these wandering netminders?
2. Which goaltender recorded the most wins in the 1980s and how many victories did he register?
3. Who was the last goalie who played in the "Original Six" to retire and when he did hang up the blades?
4. Who were the only two goalies in the 1980s to win at least 30 games three seasons in a row?
5. Three goalies won 40 games in a single season during the 1980s. Who were they and when did each reach the 40-win milestone?

6. Who led the NHL in shutouts in 1979-80 and how many zeroes did he record?

7. Which three NHL teams did Olympic hero Jim Craig play for during his brief career following the 1980 Winter Games?

8. When Pelle Lindbergh was killed in an automobile accident in 1985, the Flyers used three goaltenders to replace him. Can you name the members of the trio?

9. Name the two goalies who recorded the highest number of shutouts in a single playoff season during the 1980s. In which year did they collect their record zeros and how many did they register?

10. Name the goaltender who came within a game of equalling Gerry Cheevers' consecutive-game unbeaten streak during the 1980s and how many games did he go without suffering a loss?

11. Which goaltender had the longest winning streak during the 1980s, and how many games did he win?

12. This goaltender played all seven WHA seasons and was still active in the NHL when the 1980s came to a close. Who is he and which organization was he with when the 1988-89 season ended?

13. Who had the most single-season shutouts during the 1980s and how many zeroes did he rack up?

14. The first goalie to score a goal in professional hockey history finished his career with the Quebec Nordiques in 1982. Who was he?

15. Name the only goalie to play on a Memorial Cup winner and a Calder Cup winner in the 1980s who later played with a Stanley Cup victor in the 1990s.

16. Which NHL team used six goaltenders in the 1988-89 season?

17. Which goalie in the 1980s faced two penalty shots in the same game and what was the result?

18. Name the great goalie who recorded 355 career victories but has yet to find a berth in the Hockey Hall of Fame.

19. Who was the first goalie in NHL history to shoot the puck the length of the ice to score a goal?

20. Which former NHL goaltender was credited with scoring a goal in 1979-80?

21. Who holds the record for most games played in a single season by a goaltender and how many times did he appear between the pipes?

22. Name the only NHL goaltender to go to Europe from American college hockey before making his North American professional debut.

23. Who was the only NHL goalie to record one or more shutouts from 1979-80 through 1988-89?

24. Who was the only goalie to play at least 20 minutes in the NHL during the 1980s and not allow a goal?

25. Which goalie holds the NHL record for penalty minutes in one season?

26. During the 1980s, this netminder became the first goalie in NHL history to play for three teams in one season. Who was he?

27. Which goalie won the Vezina Trophy in a season in which he didn't record a single shutout?

28. Who was the first goaltender to win the NHL's Masterton Trophy, awarded to the player who best exemplifies the qualities of perseverance, sportsmanship, and dedication to hockey?

29. Which goalie holds the Stanley Cup record for most games in one playoff year?

30. Which goalie holds the record for most career playoff appearances in the 1980s?

31. Name the goalie who wore uniform 00 during the 1982-83 season.

32. Ron Hextall of the Flyers is the only goalie in NHL history to score a shorthanded goal in the play-offs. Against which team did he score and what was the final score of the match?

33. This Buffalo goalie became the eighteenth net-minder to record a shutout in his first NHL game. Who was he and which team did he blank?

34. This goaltender went undefeated at home during the 1988-89 season. Do you know his name and his at-home record?

35. In 1981, Dino Ciccarelli and Rick Vaive became the first players in Minnesota and Toronto history to score 50 goals in a season. Name the goalie who allowed both goals.

36. Which goalie was awarded a goal in November, 1987, only to have it taken away a few days later?

37. Six former goaltenders served as NHL general managers during the 1980s. How many can you remember?

38. Which future NHL goaltender became the first goalie in AHL history to shoot and score a goal?

39. During the 1980s, eight goaltenders were inducted into the Hockey Hall of Fame. Of these eight, one never played in the National Hockey League. Can you name the non-NHL goaltender and the circumstances surrounding his enshrinement.

40. Many NHL players have seen their offspring follow their paths to professional hockey. In the 1980s, two former NHL goaltenders saw their sons complete their NHL careers. Name the father and son duos.

Answers

1. Pat Riggin (Atlanta/Calgary, Washington, Boston and Pittsburgh), Glen Hanlon (Vancouver, St. Louis, New York Rangers, Detroit), Bob Sauve (Buffalo, Detroit, Chicago, and New Jersey) and Lindsay Middlebrook (Winnipeg, Minnesota, New Jersey, and Edmonton).

2. Mike Liut, who split the decade with St. Louis and Hartford, won 251 games during the 1980s.

3. Rogatien Vachon, who played 19 games with the Montreal Canadiens prior to expansion, retired after appearing in 38 games for the Detroit Red Wings during the 1981-82 season.

4. Ron Hextall won 37, 30, and 30 games for the Philadelphia Flyers from 1986-87 to 1988-89.

Mike Vernon won 30, 39, and 37 games for Calgary from 1986-87 to 1988-89.

5. Pete Peeters won 40 games for Boston in 1982-83; Pelle Lindbergh won 40 games for Philadelphia in 1984-85; Grant Fuhr won 40 for the Edmonton Oilers in 1987-88.

6. Tony Esposito registered six shutouts for the Blackhawks during the 1979-80 campaign, the fourth-highest total of his career.

7. Craig started his career with Atlanta before moving on to Boston and Minnesota. He also returned to the U.S. National Team in 1983, where he had an excellent 2.64 GAA with a pair of shutouts.

8. The Flyers, who, despite losing Lindbergh, won the Jennings Trophy for allowing the fewest goals against, used Bob Froese, Darren Jensen, and Chico Resch for the remainder of the 1985-86 campaign.

9. Steve Penney had three shutouts for the Montreal Canadiens in the 1984 playoffs while Pelle Lindbergh blanked the opposition three times during the 1985-86 playoffs.

10. Pete Peeters, who compiled a 27-game unbeaten streak in 1979-80 with the Philadelphia Flyers, went unbeaten in 31 straight games in 1982-83 for the Bruins. His first victory was a 5-3 win over Quebec and his unbeaten string ended with a 3-1 loss to Buffalo. Ironically, Peeters' coach at the time was Gerry Cheevers.

11. Don Beaupre won 14 straight games for the

Minnesota North Stars in the 1985-86 season. Beaupre's streak started with an 8-7 overtime victory over Toronto on February 6 and ended with a 5-4 loss to the Edmonton Oilers on March 21.

12. "King" Richard Brodeur played professionally, variously, for Quebec (WHA), Maine (AHL), New York Islanders (NHL), Vancouver (NHL), Fredericton (AHL), Hartford (NHL), and Binghamton (AHL) from 1972 to 1989. He was a member of the Hartford Whalers' organization when he retired in 1989.

13. Pete Peeters blanked the opposition eight times in 1982-83, the highest total of the decade.

14. Michel Plasse, who played with Montreal, St. Louis, Kansas City, Pittsburgh, Colorado, and Quebec, was the first professional goalie to actually shoot and score a goal. On February 21, 1971, while playing with the Kansas City Blues, Plasse shot the puck the length of the ice into the vacated Oklahoma City Blazers' cage.

15. Wendel Young played for the Memorial Cup champion Kitchener Rangers in 1982, the Calder Cup champion Hershey Bears in 1988, and the Stanley Cup champion Pittsburgh Penguins in 1991.

16. Buffalo Sabres used Clint Malarchuk, Daren Puppa, Jacques Cloutier, Darcy Wakaluk, Tom Barrasso, and Darren Eliot. The majority of games were played by Daren Puppa (37) and Jacques Cloutier (36).

17. Corrado Micalef of Detroit stopped two penalty

shots, one each by Pierre Larouche and Mike Ridley, but both players later scored goals in a 3-1 Rangers' victory in New York on February 16, 1987.

18. Rogie Vachon had a record of 355-291-115 in 795 games during his 16-year NHL career with Montreal, Los Angeles, Detroit, and Boston.

19. Ron Hextall scored for Philadelphia on December 8, 1987, against Boston in a 5-2 Flyers' win at the Spectrum.

20. The New York Islanders' Billy Smith got credit for a goal against Colorado on November 28, 1979, in a 7-4 Islanders loss.

21. Edmonton's Grant Fuhr appeared in 75 games in 1986-87, compiling a 40-24-9 record for the Oilers.

22. Tom Draper spent the 1987-88 season with Tappara of the Finnish National League before making his NHL debut with Buffalo in 1988-89.

23. Mike Liut had a total of 20 shutouts between 1980 and 1989, with at least one each year while playing for St. Louis, Hartford, and Washington.

24. Chris Clifford, who made his NHL debut with Chicago in 1984-85 and later made his second appearance in 1988-89, never allowed a goal in his brief (24-minute) NHL career.

25. Ron Hextall set the record with 113 penalty minutes while with Philadelphia in 1988-89.

26. Jim Rutherford became the first goalie in NHL history to play for three teams in one season, when he led the Kings to a 7-5 win at Winnipeg March 22, 1981. Rutherford had started the 1980-81

season with Detroit before being traded to Toronto, who later sent the well-travelled veteran to Los Angeles March 10, 1981.

27. Billy Smith won the Vezina in 1981-82 as a member of the New York Islanders. He record was 32-9-4, with no shutouts.

28. Colorado Rockies' Glenn Resch was the first goalie to win the NHL's Masterton Trophy. He won the award in 1982, after 13 forwards and one defenceman (Serge Savard) had taken it home the previous 14 years.

29. Ron Hextall of the Philadelphia Flyers appeared in a record 26 games during the 1987 playoffs.

30. Billy Smith played in a total of 102 post-season games between 1980 and 1989.

31. John Davidson wore 00 with the New York Rangers for the 1982-83 season.

32. Ron Hextall became the first goalie in NHL history to score a goal in Stanley Cup competition on April 11, 1989. Hextall's shorthanded empty-net goal gave the Flyers an 8-5 win, and a 3-2 lead in the series with the Capitals.

33. Daren Puppa played his first NHL game and recorded his first NHL shutout as the Sabres blanked Edmonton 2-0. Puppa made 37 saves, including 10 on Wayne Gretzky.

34. Montreal goalie Patrick Roy completed an unbeaten season at home, going 25-0-4, as the Canadiens tied the Flyers 2-2 on April 1, 1988.

35. Mike Liut, the NHL's First Team All-Star goalie

in 1980-81, allowed Ciccarelli's 50th goal on March 8, 1981, and surrendered Vaive's milestone marker on March 24, 1981.

36. New York Rangers' goalie Bob Froese was credited with a goal during a delayed penalty against the Islanders on November 29, 1987, but the scoring was changed a few days later when a replay revealed that Froese was not the last Ranger to touch the puck. Nine days later, on December 8, Ron Hextall became the first NHL goalie to actually shoot and score a goal.

37. Eddie Johnston (Pittsburgh, Hartford), Emile Francis (Hartford), Rogie Vachon (Los Angeles), Roger Crozier (Washington), Tony Esposito (Pittsburgh), and Gerry McNamara (Toronto) all served as NHL general managers.

38. Darcy Wakaluk, who appeared in six games for the Buffalo Sabres during the 1988-89 season, shot and scored a goal into an empty net at 19:59 of the third period to give the Rochester Americans a 5-2 win over Utica Devils on December 5, 1987. Three days later Philadelphia's Ron Hextall became the first NHL goaltender to score a goal.

39. During the 1980s, eight goaltenders entered the Hockey Hall of Fame: Lorne "Gump" Worsley and Harry Lumley (1980), Ken Dryden (1983), Bernie Parent (1984), Gerry Cheevers (1985), Ed Giacomin (1987), and Tony Esposito (1988). In 1989, the former Soviet National Team goal-

tender Vladislav Tretiak, was inducted into the Hall of Fame because of his outstanding play in international competition.

40. Pete LoPresti was the first to follow his father, former Blackhawks netminder Sam LoPresti, to the big leagues. He finished his career in 1980-81 with the Oilers. Pat Riggin ended his NHL stint with Pittsburgh in 1987-88. Dennis Riggin had a brief stay with Detroit in the late 1950s and early 1960s.

Goalies, Gee!

Match the following goaltenders with the only number they wore during their tenure with the team listed. Answers on page 135.

Murray Bannerman, Chicago   1

Greg Millen, St. Louis   29

Steve Penney, Montreal   33

Mike Liut, Hartford   37

John Vanbiesbrouck, NY Rangers   30

Don Beaupre, Minnesota   34

ACROSS

1. Pictured player.
4. Islanders' first choice in 1983 Entry Draft.
12. Original Islander coached Calgary to Cup win. (initials)
14. Former Islander shares first name with "Gump."
15. To obstruct or impede the progress of an opponent. (plural)
16. This state's university hockey team is called the Fighting Sioux.
17. Number worn by Mark Messier. (roman numeral)
18. First general manager of Islanders.
19. Defenceman scored first goal in Oilers' history.
20. Opposite of fall.
21. Brother of Denis also played with Islanders. (initials)
22. Oilers scout Garnet Bailey.
23. Swedish born defenceman with Islanders. (initials)
25. Brent and Duane had twin brothers. (initials)
26. Ex-Capitals defenceman with Islanders. (intials)
28. Playoff games played leader in Islanders' history.
31. Only Islanders goaltender on all four Cup winners.
33. One shortform for number.
34. Former Sabre became captain of Oilers. (initials)
36. Former Oiler scored 70 goals with Kings. (initials)
37. Seasons Messier played with Oilers.
38. 1989 Oilers' acquisition led Senators in scoring in '92-93. (initials)
40. Scored Stanley Cup winning goal in 1980. (initials)
41. Right-winger preceded Mike Bossy's first selection on First Team All-Stars.
42. Number worn by Mike Bossy (roman numeral)
43. 1980s Leaf led Oilers in scoring in '91-92 season. (initials)
47. He had two shutouts vs. Islanders in 1977 series.
51. Long-time Islanders coach.
55. Number of defenceman with Islanders. (intials)

Cups won by Coffey with Oilers. (roman numeral)
56. Rule reinstated this in '83-84 season. (initials)
57. Czech player began career with Oilers. (initials)
58. First name of 13 DOWN.
59. Formerly with Cleveland Barons, was on four Cup winners with Islanders. (initials)
60. With Blues in '92-93, 1980's Islander is son of Hank. (initials)
61. On '79 Cup winner with Montreal and '85 Cup winner with Edmonton. (initials)
62. Finnish-born player began NHL career with Oilers. (initials)
66. Led NHL in goalscoring in '85-86 season.
69. Won Norris Trophy in '84-85 and '85-86.
70. Oilers' goaltender won Conn Smythe Trophy.

DOWN

1. Third coach in Oilers' history.
2. Bossy tied his 50 goals in 50 games record.
3. First Islanders' captain became Islanders broadcaster.
4. 1980's Oiler became first Senators' captain.
5. Defeated in 1980 Cup final.
6. Oilers joined this league for '79-80 season. (initials)
7. Chicago goaltender made final playoff appearance in '83. (initials)
8. All-time leader for Oilers in powerplay goals.
9. Opposite of out.
10. Two of these form Wayne's number.
11. Opposite of beginning.
13. First captain of NHL Oilers.
24. Islanders defenceman taken by Oilers in expansion draft. (initials)
26. Chico's given first name.
27. Holds Oilers' consecutive games played streak. (initials)
29. Hart winner with Isles.
30. Player not working or not active.
31. Cowboy

played with Oilers. (initials)

32. Number of minutes in regulation time.

35. Rat.

39. 1988 Oiler draft pick traded to Quebec in '93. (initials)

44. Finnish defenceman with Oilers. (initials)

45. Small centreman was member

of '88 Cup winners. (initials)

46. Ironman ended NHL career with Oilers. (initials)

48. Hunter brother played for Oilers.

49. This King among Islanders.

50. Seasons Gretzky played with Oilers.

52. Oilers goaltender.

53. Played 12 seasons with Islanders, later played with Kings.

54. Butch's given first name.

63. Opposite of short.

64. Number of Cup finals Oilers have played in. (roman numeral)

65. Opposite of on.

66. To disagree or clash with another.

67. Most notable King traded in Gretzky trade.

68. Only goaltender Islanders faced in '82 Cup finals. (initials)

Solution on pages 137-138

⑨

Swap Shop: Trades and Transactions in the 1980s

THE DECADE OF THE 1980S SAW MORE MAJOR TRANSAC-
tions involving "franchise" players than any previous ten-year period. Seven teams – Toronto,
Los Angeles, Edmonton, Minnesota, Calgary,
Washington, and St. Louis – traded their all-time
leading scorers in the 1980s, while many others
swapped big-name stars to other organizations. The
decision to pull the trigger on a trade involving a
franchise mainstay is always difficult, but a general
manager's job is made up of such choices, of trying to
receive some return for an investment while the
player in question still has market value.

This reasoning gave us the "deal of the century"
in 1988 that sent Wayne Gretzky to the Los Angeles
Kings from the Edmonton Oilers. Fans in Edmonton
and elsewhere were upset at the time of the deal, but
the Oilers returned to the winner's circle only one

year after the Gretzky trade. Similar outpourings of emotion were felt in St. Louis when Bernie Federko was sent to Detroit, and in Toronto when two favourites, Lanny McDonald and Darryl Sittler, were dispatched to other teams.

Another trade that shocked fans involved Butch Goring, one of the Los Angeles Kings' most popular players, who proved to be the missing ingredient in the New York Islanders' Stanley Cup recipe. Rich in talent but somehow unable to get over the top, the Islanders sent Billy Harris and Dave Lewis to the Kings in 1980 to acquire the tenacious Goring, whose work ethic and special-teams expertise helped lead the Islanders to four Stanley Cup titles.

The Washington Capitals improved when they acquired defenceman Rod Langway from the Montreal Canadiens. The Caps had missed the play-offs in every year of their existence, but with Langway aboard, they finished second in the Patrick Division five times and first once.

In 1989, the Calgary Flames finally won their first championship, with three players from the St. Louis Blues playing key roles. Calgary GM Cliff Fletcher acquired Rob Ramage, Doug Gilmour, and Rick Wamsley in a pair of deals that brought Stanley Cup success to the Flames. The price was steep, however, for a prospect named Brett Hull was included in the trade that brought Ramage and Wamsley to Calgary. Hull is now one of the league's dominant marksman, while Ramage, Gilmour, and Wamsley are no longer with the Flames'.

Major trades including Marcel Dionne, Kent Nilsson, Dino Ciccarelli, Bobby Smith, Paul Coffey, Tom Barrasso, Adam Oates, and Mike Gartner were also consummated in the 1980s. Two other transactions stand out. The Boston Bruins sent Barry Pederson to Vancouver for Cam Neely. Pederson never regained the form he showed with Boston while Neely became the Bruins' offensive leader. Vancouver also sent Patrik Sundstrom to New Jersey for Greg Adams and Kirk McLean, two players who are now cornerstones of the Canucks franchise.

The swap shop is still open in the 1990s, with many more marquee names going on the trading block. New Jersey, the Islanders, Montreal, Winnipeg, and Chicago have all seen "franchise" players join other teams. The down side to this is the wear and tear on fan loyalty; sometimes it seems that no sooner is a player winning the affection and admiration of hometown fans than he's part of a radical swap. The bright side to constant player movement is that it allows teams which make good trades to improve rapidly, thereby making the NHL increasingly competitive.

Questions

1. In a controversial trade, this All-Star sniper was traded to the L.A. Kings for a draft choice. The player involved played only 27 games for the Kings while the draft selection became a dominant player in the league. Name the player

traded and the player acquired with the Kings' draft selection.

2. In the 1980s, two players were selected in the NHL's entry draft who later went on to play major-league baseball. Who were they?

3. Name the ten players selected first overall in each of the NHL's entry drafts from 1980 to 1989.

4. Two players selected in the first round of the 1980 Entry Draft have already compiled 1,000 career points. Who are they?

5. Before he left the Montreal Canadiens organization, Sam Pollock traded two players to Colorado for the Rockies' first selection in the 1980 Entry Draft, which eventually turned out to be the first selection overall. Who did the Rockies receive in return for their number one draft choice and when was the deal made?

6. In 1988, Calgary GM Cliff Fletcher dealt Brett Hull to St. Louis for two players he hoped would contribute to a Stanley Cup championship. Which players did the Flames receive and who was the second player dispatched to St. Louis with the Golden Brett?

7. In the 1980 Entry Draft, the Montreal Canadiens were criticized for passing over hometown talent Denis Savard for western junior Doug Wickenheiser. The Winnipeg Jets also had a shot at selecting Savard, but chose this player instead. Who is he?

8. In the 1980s, five goaltenders were drafted in the first round. Can you recall their names?

9. In 1987, the Vancouver Canucks, who finished in last place in the Smythe Division, swung a deal with the New Jersey Devils that solidified their future. Can you name the two players the Canucks received and the record-setting player they dispatched to the Devils?

10. In 1989, the St. Louis Blues infuriated their fans by trading two favourites to Detroit, although the trade was highly beneficial for the Blues and a disaster for the Wings. Who were the four players involved in the deal?

11. In the 1980s, three first-overall draft picks were chosen from outside the Canadian major junior system. Who are the three players and where were they drafted from?

12. Who was the future NHLer who was once traded for a bus when he was in junior?

13. On July 21, 1981, the Colorado Rockies signed a Boston Bruins player as a free agent. As part of the compensation, the Bruins received the Rockies' first selection in the 1982 Entry Draft, which turned out to be the first choice overall. The Bruins then acquired two players from the Minnesota North Stars for not selecting Brian Bellows. Which player did the Rockies sign as a free agent from the Bruins and which two players did Boston receive from Minnesota?

14. Other than the Colorado Rockies, only one other team traded a first-round pick that ended up being the first overall selection. Which team traded the pick and which team acquired it?

15. Marcel Dionne, the NHL's third all-time leading scorer, was traded to the New York Rangers in 1987 in a four-player transaction. Who were the three other players involved?

16. Which former NHL coach was once "traded" for $100,000 and a first-round draft choice?

17. Which two NHL GMs of the 1980s had both been first-round draft picks of the Montreal Canadiens?

18. Name the two brothers who were selected highest overall in the NHL entry draft?

19. Which NHL team did not participate in the 1983 Entry Draft?

20. The last player chosen in the 1980 Entry Draft (210th overall) played in the NHL throughout the 1980s. Can you name him?

21. Who was the oldest player ever selected in the NHL entry draft?

22. Who was the only U.S. high school player selected in the first round of the 1982 NHL draft?

23. Which veteran defenceman was traded twice for a Norris Trophy winner?

24. This player was drafted ninth overall in the 1975 Amateur Draft by Montreal but decided not to play pro hockey. In 1988, he re-emerged as a key performer on the 1988 Austrian Olympic Team. Who is he?

25. Who was the first U.S.-born player to be selected first overall in the NHL entry draft?

26. Bobby Hull was traded only once during his career. Which team acquired him, which team

traded him, and which number did he wear with his new team?

27. In one of the decade's most one-sided trades, the Boston Bruins sent Barry Pederson to Vancouver in exchange for a player and a first-round draft choice in the 1987 Entry Draft. Who was the player and which player did the Bruins select?

28. Which non-goalie was drafted in the first round of the NHL draft, despite scoring no goals in 70 games the year he was drafted?

29. Name the two teams who exchanged their number-one goalies in 1980 and name the goalies involved.

30. Which two players did the Edmonton Oilers receive in exchange for Andy Moog in March, 1988?

31. Which three players did Montreal send to Minnesota to acquire Bobby Smith?

32. In 1980, the Buffalo Sabres sent this player to the L.A. Kings for the draft selection they would use to select Phil Housley. Who was the player the Sabres sent to the Kings?

33. On September 17, 1979, the Atlanta Flames signed one of the heroes of Team Canada 1972 "Series of the Century" squad. He made his first appearance in the NHL since 1974. Who was he?

34. On November 2, 1979, the New York Rangers traded four players and a draft choice to Colorado to acquire this player. Who did the Rangers receive and who did they send to the Rockies?

35. In February 1980, the Vancouver Canucks traded their all-time leading scorer to Atlanta to receive a player the Flames had acquired one year earlier. Who were the principals involved?

36. This prospect, drafted by St. Louis in 1989, became the first player to be drafted twice, when the Washington Capitals also chose him in the 1991 Entry Draft. Who was he and how could he have been selected twice?

37. In 1985, the annual NHL entry draft was held outside of Montreal for the first time. Name the location and the first player selected.

38. In 1983, five American-born players were selected in the opening round of the NHL entry draft, an NHL record at the time. Name the U.S. prospects?

39. In 1985, four goalies were picked in the second round of the NHL Entry Draft. Can you name the goaltenders, their amateur teams, and the NHL teams which selected them?

40. During the 1980s, thirteen U.S. high-school prospects were selected in the first round of the NHL Entry Draft. Of the thirteen, only two of the prospects never played in the NHL. Ironically, the same team selected both of them. Name the two players and the team.

Answers

1. The Sabres' Rick Martin was sent to the Kings for

L.A.'s first selection in the 1983 Entry Draft, which turned out to be Tom Barrasso.

2. The Winnipeg Jets selected Kirk McCaskill (California Angels, Chicago White Sox) 64th overall in the 1981 Entry Draft. The L.A. Kings chose Tom Glavine (Atlanta Braves) 69th overall in 1984.

3. First picks during the 1980s: Doug Wickenheiser (Montreal, 1980), Dale Hawerchuk (Winnipeg, 1981), Gord Kluzak (Boston, 1982), Brian Lawton (Minnesota, 1983), Mario Lemieux (Pittsburgh, 1984), Wendel Clark (Toronto, 1985), Joe Murphy (Detroit, 1986), Pierre Turgeon (New York Islanders, 1987), Mike Modano (Minnesota, 1988) and Mats Sundin (Quebec, 1989).

4. Denis Savard reached the 1,000-point plateau on March 11, 1990 with the Blackhawks, while Paul Coffey hit the 1,000-point mark on December 22, 1990 with the Penguins.

5. The Canadiens sent Ron Andruff and Sean Shanahan to the Rockies, plus an exchange of first-round choices, for the Rockies' first selection. The deal was completed on September 13, 1976, a full four years before the draft. Pollock had his eye on a young junior named Denis Savard, but his successors (Ron Caron, Irving Grundman) chose Doug Wickenheiser from the Regina Pats of the WHL over Savard. Interestingly, throughout Pollock's career, he never made a first-round selection from the Western league.

6. Calgary sent Steve Bozek and Hull to the Blues for Rob Ramage and Rick Wamsley, both of whom played key roles in Calgary's 1989 championship season.

7. The Jets chose defenceman Dave Babych, who represented Winnipeg in the NHL All-Star Games of 1983 and 1984.

8. Grant Fuhr (8th overall, 1981), Tom Barrasso (5th overall, 1983), Jimmy Waite (8th overall, 1987), Jason Muzzatti (21st overall, 1988), and Olaf Kolzig (19th overall, 1989) are the first-round goalies.

9. On September 15, 1987, the Devils sent goaltender Kirk McLean and centre Greg Adams to the Canucks for Patrik Sundstrom, who went on to become the first player to record eight points in a playoff game.

10. The Blues sent all-time leading scorer Bernie Federko and Tony McKegney to Detroit for Adam Oates and Paul MacLean. Federko played only one season, while McKegney lasted only 14 games. Oates became a perennial 100-point player and the league's finest playmaker with the St. Louis Blues.

11. Brain Lawton (Mount St. Charles High School), Joe Murphy (Michigan State), and Mats Sundin (Nacka, Sweden) were the only players chosen from outside the CHL.

12. In 1981, the Seattle Breakers of the WHL acquired a bus from the Victoria Cougars for cash and a player. The player was Tom Martin, who at the

time was a freshman with the University of Denver. Martin completed the deal by joining the Victoria team in 1983-84. He later played for Winnipeg, Minnesota, and Hartford in the NHL.

13. The Rockies signed Dwight Foster (who played a total of 74 games with the club) as a free agent and lost the right to draft first overall. Kluzak, Bellows, Scott Stevens, and Phil Housley were all available. Minnesota sent Dave Donnelly and Brad Palmer to Boston for the Bruins' promise not to select Brian Bellows. The Bruins later traded Donnelly to re-acquire Dwight Foster.

14. The Pittsburgh Penguins traded their first-round draft choice in 1983 to the Minnesota North Stars for Anders Hakansson, Ron Meighan, and a switch of first-round draft choices for George Ferguson. The North Stars chose Brian Lawton and the Penguins took Bob Errey.

15. The Kings sent Dionne and defenceman Jeff Crossman to the Rangers for Bobby Carpenter and defenceman Tom Laidlaw.

16. The New York Rangers' GM Phil Esposito "traded" $100,000 and a 1988 first-round pick to the Quebec Nordiques for their coach, Michel Bergeron, on June 18, 1987. The Nordiques later used the pick to select Daniel Dore.

17. Bob Gainey (1973, 8th overall), the current GM of the Dallas Stars, and Doug Risebrough (1974, 7th overall), the current GM of the Calgary Flames, were both former stars with *les Canadiens*.

18. Pierre Turgeon was chosen first overall in 1987

by Buffalo, and brother Sylvain was chosen second overall in 1983 by Hartford.

19. The St. Louis Blues missed the entire 1983 Entry Draft due to difficulties resulting from a change of ownership.

20. Andy Brickley began his career in 1982-83 and has played for Philadelphia, Pittsburgh, New Jersey, and Boston.

21. Helmut Balderis was 37 years old when he was drafted by Minnesota in 1989 and had not played in four years after 11 seasons in the USSR.

22. Phil Housley was selected sixth overall by Buffalo out of South St. Paul High School in Minnesota where he had 65 points in 22 games.

23. Moe Mantha was traded to Pittsburgh from Winnipeg for 1981 Norris winner Randy Carlyle on May 1, 1984, and to Edmonton from Pittsburgh for two-time Norris winner Paul Coffey on November 24, 1987.

24. Robin Sadler was the top prospect who walked out on the both the Montreal Canadiens and the Edmonton Oilers.

25. Brian Lawton, who was born in New Brunswick, New Jersey, was selected first overall by Minnesota in 1983.

26. On February 27, 1980, Bobby Hull was traded to the Hartford Whalers from the Winnipeg Jets for "future considerations." With the Whalers he wore number 16 because his customary number 9 was being worn by someone named Howe.

27. The Bruins received Cam Neely and Vancouver's

first-round choice in the 1987 Entry Draft, which they used to select Glen Wesley.

28. Jeff Beukeboom, selected 19th overall in 1983 by the Edmonton Oilers, failed to score a goal in 70 OHL games the previous season.

29. On July 15, 1980, the Boston Bruins sent Gilles Gilbert to the Detroit Red Wings for Rogie Vachon.

30. The Edmonton Oilers acquired goalie Bill Ranford and Geoff Courtnall from the Boston Bruins in exchange for Andy Moog.

31. The North Stars received Keith Acton, Mark Napier, and a draft selection, which turned out to be Ken Hodge, Jr., for one of the NHL's classiest players, Bobby Smith.

32. On March 10, 1980, the Sabres traded defenceman Jerry Korab to Los Angeles in exchange for the Kings' first-round pick in 1982. That pick was used to select Phil Housley.

33. The Flames signed free agent Paul Henderson, who played, variously, with Toronto and Birmingham in the WHA from 1974 to 1979.

34. The New York Rangers obtained defenceman Barry Beck from the Colorado Rockies in exchange for Lucien DeBlois, Pat Hickey, Mike McEwen, Dean Turner, and future considerations (Bobby Crawford).

35. On February 8, 1980, Vancouver sent Don Lever, their all-time leading goal (186) and point (407) scorer, and winger Brad Smith to Atlanta for centre Ivan Boldirev and left winger Darcy Rota.

36. Rick Corriveau, drafted 31st overall by St. Louis in 1989, decided not to sign with the Blues and re-entered the draft as an overage junior in 1991. Washington selected him in the eighth round, 168th overall.

37. The 1985 NHL Entry Draft was held in the Metro Toronto Convention Centre, where the Maple Leafs selected Wendel Clark as the first overall pick.

38. Brian Lawton, Pat LaFontaine, Tom Barrasso, Alfie Turcotte, and David Jensen were the five U.S. players selected in the first round of the 1983 Entry Draft.

39. In round two of the 1985 Entry Draft, a record four goaltenders were selected, three of them being chosen consecutively. New Jersey, picking 24th, chose Sean Burke from the Toronto Marlboros. Next, Medicine Hat's Troy Gamble was picked by Vancouver. The Whalers made it a "goalie hat-trick" with Peterborough Pete's Kay Whitmore. The New York Rangers selected U.S. high-school star Mike Richter 28th overall.

40. The Calgary Flames made both selections. In 1985, the Flames chose Chris Biotti, who never made it beyond the IHL. In 1986, the team selected Minnesota high-school prospect George Pelawa, who was killed in a motor vehicle accident before entering university.

Draftees

The following players were taken in the 1983 Entry Draft. Match the player's name with his selection number on the right. Answers on page 135.

Peter Zezel	26th overall
Bob Essensa	41st overall
Tom Barrasso	121st overall
Rick Tocchet	214th overall
Uwe Krupp	5th overall
Claude Lemieux	69th overall

The Dynasties

The Edmonton Oilers and the New York Islanders dominated the decade of the 1980s, winning four championships each with lineups that were laden with All-Star talent. The Islanders were built slowly and deliberately through the NHL's amateur and entry draft. (Note: the NHL's amateur draft was renamed the entry draft in 1979.) The Isles won their first championship in 1980 after several years of playoff frustration. Despite some early-round eliminations in the late 1970s, the Islanders stayed with their personnel, confident they would eventually succeed. The Oilers were built through the entry draft, trades, and free-agent signings, always building with an eye to youth, speed, and offence. The Oilers won their first title in only their fifth NHL season, but also had to overcome bitter playoff defeats in 1982 and 1983.

The New York Islanders, who replaced the Montreal Canadiens as the league's dominant franchise in 1980, were constructed using a blueprint very similar to that of *les glorieux*. Meticulously built using draft choices and clever transactions, the Islanders captured four consecutive Stanley Cups from 1980 to 1983. Sixteen players appeared on all four Cup winners, the most of any dynasty team in league history. Only minor adjustments were made along the way. Many of the players who were the backbone of the Islanders' success – Bossy, Potvin, Nystrom, Morrow, Persson – played their entire careers with the team. Others, like Billy Smith, who began his career with the Kings, and Bryan Trottier, who finished his with Pittsburgh, enjoyed lengthy stays on Long Island.

The Edmonton Oilers, molded around the talents of Wayne Gretzky, Mark Messier, Glenn Anderson, Jari Kurri, Paul Coffey, and Grant Fuhr, won four Cups in five years by incessantly rearranging their lineup. While the core was stable, the rest of the lineup was was subject to considerable turnover, especially as playoffs drew near, with Glen Sather mixing in talented veterans and European specialists, such as Reijo Ruotsalainen, Kent Nilsson, Willy Lindstrom, and Jaroslav Pouzar.

Unlike the Islanders, the Oilers realized that the key to their continuing dominance was to change personnel. After losing to Calgary in the 1986 play-offs, the Oilers made numerous line-up changes, adding Craig McTavish, Jeff Beukeboom, Kelly

Buchberger, and Moe Lemay. The following year, newcomers Keith Acton, Geoff Courtnall, Dave Hannan, and Normand Lacombe were added. The results? The Oilers won their fourth championship in five years.

The Islanders, by contrast, were reluctant to part with their marquee players, seemingly content to retain many from their championship season instead of restructuring. As a result, the team finished in sixth place in the Patrick Division in 1988. The Oilers, on the other hand, traded away many of their star players while they still held market value and used the resulting new acquisitions to capture their fifth Cup championship in 1990.

Questions

1. Which player, who was a member of all four New York Islander Cup-winning teams in the 1980s, was also a member of the WHA's Edmonton Oilers?
2. Name the two men who coached the Islanders in the 1980s.
3. Who scored the winning goal in the Edmonton Oilers' first-ever playoff victory and against which team?
4. Only one player won the Stanley Cup with both the Edmonton Oilers and the New York Islanders in the 1980s. Who was he?

5. Name two players on the Oilers' Stanley Cup-winning team in 1985 who were members of the Montreal Canadiens' Cup-winners in 1979.

6. When the New York Islanders won the Cup in 1979-80, four players had been with the team since the club's first season in 1972. Who were the veteran Islanders?

7. How many goals did the Edmonton Oilers score in the first three rounds of the 1983 playoffs and how many did they score in the finals?

8. In the opening game of the 1984 finals, the Edmonton Oilers shocked the New York Islanders with a 1-0 victory. Who scored the winning goal and who was the winning goaltender?

9. Which three goaltenders did the New York Islanders use during the 1979-80 season?

10. During their first NHL season, the Oilers used six goaltenders, three of whom never played in the NHL again. Of those three, one was a former New York Islander product, one was a former WHA goalie who led the league in shutouts in 1978-79 and the other a member of the 1980 Canadian Olympic Team. How many of the six can you name?

11. Glen Sather was the first coach of the Oilers and John Muckler the third. Name the second.

12. In the 1980s, nine teams rebounded from 2-0 and/or 3-1 deficits in games to win a playoff round. However, only the New York Islanders came back to win one series they trailed 2-0 and another they trailed 3-1. Who were the teams the

Islanders defeated and in which years did the comebacks occur?

13. The Philadelphia Flyers were awarded a penalty shot in consecutive games in the 1985 Stanley Cup finals versus the Edmonton Oilers. Who took the shots for Philly, who was in net for the Oilers, and what was the result?

14. Two players on the 1972-73 WHA Alberta Oilers were also members of the first Edmonton Oilers team in the NHL. Who were they?

15. Each of the first three draft selections of the Edmonton Oilers in the 1979 Entry Draft went on to play on every Cup winner in the 1980s. Name the well-scouted trio.

16. In 1982, the Oilers played the highest-scoring game in Stanley Cup history. What was the final score and who were the Oilers' opponents?

17. Which Edmonton Oiler star holds the record for scoring the fastest two shorthanded goals in NHL history?

18. This New York Islander set an NHL record in 1981 with points in 18 consecutive playoff games. Who was he?

19. Who scored the first goal in the NHL history of the Edmonton Oilers?

20. In a November 28, 1979 game against the Rockies, Billy Smith became the first goalie in NHL history to get credit for a goal. Who was the Colorado player who shot the puck into his own net?

21. On February 20, 1982, the New York Islanders set

an NHL record with their 15th consecutive victory. Which team did they defeat for the milestone victory and who scored the winning goal?

22. Which member of the Edmonton Oilers holds the franchise record for most consecutive games played scoring at least one goal per game?

23. Who scored the first hat-trick in the history of the Edmonton Oilers franchise?

24. Who recorded the first shutout in Edmonton Oilers' history and which team was blanked?

25. Which goalie surrendered Mike Bossy's milestone 50th goal in his 50th game during the 1980-81 season?

26. Name the All-Star Oilers defenceman who was drafted off the roster of a Japanese club known as the Kikudo Bunnies?

27. On April 12, 1986, Mike Bossy became the NHL's all-time leading playoff goal scorer. Whose record did he break and how many playoff goals did he score in his career?

28. On April 6, 1988, Denis Potvin established a new record for playoff games played. Whose record did Potvin break?

29. When the Edmonton Oilers captured their first Stanley Cup title in 1984, four different marksmen scored the game-winning goals in the series. Who were they?

30. This NHL coach had already been fired by two teams in the same season when the Oilers hired him to help them in the 1984 playoffs. Who was he and which teams had let him go?

31. Who was the Oilers' backup goalie the night they won their first Stanley Cup?

32. Four former National Hockey League players had sons with the same name playing in the NHL in the 1980s. Of the four, only one father/son combination has had its names engraved on the Stanley Cup. The son was a member of the Oilers. Who is he and who was his father?

33. The Oilers just missed winning the Avco Cup in 1978-79, the last year of the World Hockey Association. Their first Stanley Cup championship team was loaded with ex-WHA players. Name the nine former WHAers who were part of the Edmonton Oilers' when the team won its first Stanley Cup.

34. Three players who played on the Islanders' championship teams in the 1980s have been inducted into the Hockey Hall of Fame. Name this terrific trio.

35. Despite all the great players who were members of their teams, only one jersey number was retired by either the Oilers or Islanders during the 1980s. Name the player, team, and jersey number.

Answers

1. Dave Langevin, who played for the WHA's Edmonton Oilers from 1976-77 to 1978-79, was reclaimed by the Islanders prior to the 1979

Expansion Draft and played all on all four Islander Cup winners from 1980 to 1983.

2. Al Arbour coached the team from 1979-80 to 1985-86, and again from 1988-89 to the present day. Terry Simpson was in his third year as the Islanders coach when he was relieved of his duties and replaced by Arbour.

3. Brett Callighen scored the Oilers' fourth goal in a 6-3 victory over the Montreal Canadiens in the first game of the 1981 preliminary round.

4. Billy Carroll, who won three Cups with the Islanders in 1981-83, also won a Stanley Cup with the Edmonton Oilers in 1985.

5. Pat Hughes and Mark Napier, members of the Canadiens' Cup win in 1979, were also members of the Oilers' championship team in 1985.

6. Billy Smith, drafted off the roster of the L.A. Kings in the 1972 Expansion Draft; Bob Nystrom, selected in the third round of the 1972 Amateur Draft; Lorne Henning, selected in the second round of the 1972 Amateur Draft; and Garry Howatt, chosen in the ninth round of the 1972 Amateur Draft,.

7. The Oilers scored 74 goals in only 12 playoff games after winning their first three playoff rounds 3-0, 4-1, 4-0. In the finals, the Islanders limited the Oilers to six goals in four games.

8. Kevin McClelland, with assists from Brent Hughes and Dave Hunter, won the opening game with a goal at the 1:55 mark of the third

period. Grant Fuhr stopped 34 shots to earn the shutout.

9. Billy Smith, Glenn "Chico" Resch, and Richard Brodeur were the trio of netminders utilized by the Islanders in their first championship season.

10. Eddie Mio, Dave Dryden, and Ron Low were the top three Oiler goalies. Jim Corsi, Don Cutts, and Bob Dupuis were the other three whose NHL careers ended after the 1979-80 season.

11. Bryan Watson started the 1980-81 season as coach.

12. The Islanders fell behind the Montreal Canadiens 2-0 in the Wales Conference Finals in 1984 before winning the set in six games. In 1987, the Isles were down three games to one against the Washington Capitals before rebounding to win the set in seven games on Pat LaFontaine's goal in the fourth overtime period.

13. Ron Sutter was awarded a penalty shot at 8:47 of the first period in game four with the Flyers leading 2-1. The shot was stopped by Grant Fuhr, enabling the Oilers to outscore the Flyers 4-1 during the rest of the game to win the match 5-3. In game five, Dave Poulin was awarded a penalty shot at 12:51 of the third period with Edmonton holding a commanding 8-3 lead. Grant Fuhr stopped the shot.

14. Al Hamilton and Jim Harrison were both members of the 1972-73 Oilers and the 1979-80 Oilers.

15. Kevin Lowe (second overall), Mark Messier (48th overall), and Glenn Anderson (69th overall).

16. The L.A. Kings beat Edmonton 10-8 at Edmonton on April 7, 1982, in game one of the first round. The Kings went on to upset the Oilers in five games in the best-of-five first round.

17. Esa Tikkanen set an NHL record by scoring twice for Edmonton in just 12 seconds in a 1988-89 game against Toronto. He broke the record that had been set by former Oiler Pat Hughes. Hughes had broken the record set by Oilers' star Wayne Gretzky.

18. Bryan Trottier registered at least one point in every playoff game during the 1981 playoffs, compiling 11 goals, 18 assists, and 29 points.

19. Kevin Lowe scored the Oilers' first NHL goal in a 4-2 loss to the Chicago Blackhawks on October 10, 1979. Wayne Gretzky assisted on the goal to register his first NHL point.

20. Smith was the last Islander to touch the puck before Rob Ramage fired the puck into his own net on a delayed penalty call. The Islanders still lost the game 7-4 to the Rockies at Denver.

21. The Islanders defeated the Colorado Rockies 3-2 for their 15th straight win. John Tonelli scored the winning goal with 47 seconds left in the game.

22. Dave Lumley scored a goal in each of 12 consecutive games, from November 21, 1981 to December 16, 1981, the second longest streak since 1922.

23. On October 19, 1979, Blair MacDonald scored his first career hat-trick, and the first three-goal effort in the Oilers' NHL history, to lead

Edmonton to their first NHL victory, a 6-3 win over Quebec.

24. On December 9, 1979, Eddie Mio recorded the first shutout in the Edmonton Oilers' NHL history, a 3-0 decision over Hartford, at Northlands Coliseum in Edmonton.

25. On January 24, 1981, Bossy scored against Quebec's Ron Grahame in a 7-3 win to become only the second player in NHL history to score 50 goals in the first 50 games of a season. Maurice Richard was the first in 1944-45 season.

26. Randy Gregg, who played college hockey for the University of Alberta, played two seasons in Japan before being drafted by the Oilers.

27. Mike Bossy scored his 83rd career playoff goal to break Maurice Richard's long-held NHL record of 82. Bossy, who scored 85 post-season goals in his career, fired the record-breaker in a 3-1 Islander loss to Washington on April 12, 1986.

28. Denis Potvin broke Henri Richard's NHL record when he appeared in the 181st playoff game of his career. Larry Robinson eventually broke Potvin's mark.

29. Kevin McClelland, Glenn Anderson, Mark Messier, and Ken Linseman were the sharp-shooting Oilers who vaulted Edmonton to the Cup in 1984.

30. After being fired by both the Vancouver Canucks and the Los Angeles Kings in the same season, the Oilers hired Roger Neilson as a video coach during the 1984 playoffs.

31. Mike Zanier, who had never played a minute in the NHL, was serving as Andy Moog's backup because Grant Fuhr had an injured shoulder.
32. Lee Fogolin, Sr., was a member of the Detroit Red Wing championship team in 1949-50. Not to be outdone, Lee, Jr., was a member of the 1983-84 Oilers and proceeded to win three more Stanley Cup championships during the 1980s.
33. The Oilers' first Stanley Cup-winning team in 1983-84 had the names of nine ex-WHA players names engraved on the Cup. Led by Wayne Gretzky, the other eight names were Dave Hunter, Willy Lindstrom, Ken Linseman, Mark Messier, and Dave Semenko. From the front office were coach/general manager Glen Sather, assistant coach Ted Green, and assistant general manager Bruce MacGregor.
34. Denis Potvin (1991), Mike Bossy (1991), and "Battlin'" Billy Smith (1993) have all been honoured with induction into the Hockey Hall of Fame.
35. Only the Edmonton Oilers retired a number during the 1980s. It belonged to former WHA star defenceman Al Hamilton, who played seven seasons in the WHA and finished his career in 1979-80. He wore jersey number 3.

Answers

Page 13

1. John Tucker
2. John Ogrodnick
3. John Tonelli
4. John Kordic
5. John Chabot
6. John MacLean

Page 27

1980-81	Roland Melanson, Duane Sutter
1983-84	Randy Gregg, Charlie Huddy
1985-86	Mike Lalor, Mario Tremblay
1988-89	Hakan Loob, Mark Hunter

Page 39

Steve Larmer	1980-81
Pelle Lindbergh	1981-82
Chris Kontos	1982-83
Marty McSorley	1983-84
Joel Otto	1984-85
Bill Ranford	1985-86

Page 52

Neilson	Buffalo, 1980-81
Brooks	Minnesota, 1987-88
Murdoch	Chicago, 1987-88
Martin	St. Louis, 1986-87 to 1987-88
Angotti	Pittsburgh, 1983-84
Watt	Vancouver, 1985-86 to 1986-87

Page 77

A. 4
B. 3
C. 1
D. 5
E. 2

Page 89

Balderis	Minnesota
Summanen	Edmonton, Vancouver
Bubla	Vancouver
Hallin	NY Islanders, Minnesota
Petersson	St. Louis, Hartford, Washington
Eldebrink	Vancouver, Quebec

Page 103

Murray Bannerman	30
Greg Millen	29
Steve Penney	37
Mike Liut	1
John Vanbiesbrouck	34
Don Beaupre	33

Page 120

Peter Zezel	41st overall
Bob Essensa	69th overall
Tom Barrasso	5th overall
Rick Tocchet	121st overall
Uwe Krupp	214th overall
Claude Lemieux	26th overall

C J X U E I M E L O I R A M C
H O C K E Y Z R S A P T M O W
L H L P B F R E E A G E N T A
Y N A O E T B C M T N Q X D Y
E Z R W R F J H A I T S L H N
Y I E L N A P O L P U U V C E
S E H E I R D G F A T S S Z G
S G T J E D I O Y H G A D F R
O L A P F Y C A R E D L I N E
B E S E E R I L A O K L Z N T
E R N E D T N L G P C X C V Z
K R E A E N G I L A M K N B K
I T L L R E Y N A S U I I O Y
M H G T K G F E C S D S A E P
J K O Y O R K C I R T A P W S

Pages 104-105

1. MORROW (Ken Morrow)
4. LAFONTAINE (Pat Lafontaine)
12. TC (Terry Crisp)
14. HENNING (Lorne Henning)
15. CHECKS
16. ND (North Dakota)
17. XI (Eleven)
18. TORREY (Bill Torrey)
19. LOWE (Kevin Lowe)
20. RISE
21. JP (Jean Potvin)
22. ACE ("Ace" Bailey)
23. SP (Stefan Perrson)
25. RS (Ron & Rich Sutter)
26. GL (Gord Lane)
28. POTVIN (Denis Potvin)
31. BILLYSMITH (Billy Smith)
33. NR
34. LF (Lee Fogolin)
36. BN (Bernie Nicholls)
37. TWELVE
38. NM (Norm MacIver)
40. BN (Bob Nystrom)
41. GUY (Guy Lafleur)
42. XXII (22)
43. VD (Vincent Damphousse)
47. KENDRYDEN (Ken Dryden)
51. ALARBOUR (Al Arbour)
55. III (Three)
56. OT (overtime)
57. VR (Vladimir Ruzicka)
58. RON
59. WM (Wayne Merrick)
60. BB (Bob Bassen)
61. MN (Mark Napier)
62. ET (Esa Tikkanen)
66. JARIKURRI (Jari Kurri)
69. COFFEY (Paul Coffey)
70. BILLRANFORD (Bill Ranford)

Down

1. MUCKLER (John Muckler)
2. ROCKET (Maurice Richard)
3. WESTFALL (Ed Westfall)

4. LAURIE (Laurie Boschman)
5. FLYERS (Philadelphia Flyers)
6. NHL (National Hockey League)
7. TE (Tony Esposito)
8. ANDERSON (Glenn Anderson)
9. IN
10. NINES
11. END
13. CHIPPERFIELD (Ron Chipperfield)
24. PAT (Pat Price)
26. GLENN (Glenn Resch)
27. CM (Craig MacTavish)
29. TROTTIER (Bryan Trottier)
30. IDLE
31. BF (Bill Flett)
32. SIXTY
35. LINSEMAN (Ken Linseman)
39. MG (Martin Gelinas)
44. RR (Reijo Ruotsalainen)
45. KA (Keith Acton)
46. GU (Garry Unger)
48. DAVE (Dave Hunter)
49. DEREK (Derek King)
50. NINE
52. LOW (Ron Low)
53. BOB (Bob Bourne)
54. ROBERT
63. TALL
64. VI (Six)
65. OFF
66. JAR
67. JC (Jimmy Carson)
68. RB (Richard Brodeur)